Queering Shantideva's the Way of the Bodhisattva

DAVID FRANKLIN SPARKS

Queering Shantideva's the Way of the Bodhisattva

A Buddhist Classic in Contemporary Queer Vernacular

Publisher's Cataloging-in-Publication
(Provided by Cassidy Cataloguing Services, Inc.)

Names: Śāntideva, active 7th century, author. | Sparks, David Franklin, 1985- author, translator. | Śāntideva, active 7th century. Way of the Bodhisattva.

Title: Queering Shantideva's the Way of the Bodhisattva : a Buddhist classic in contemporary queer vernacular / David Franklin Sparks.

Description: Second edition. | Lexington, Kentucky : dFRAE, [2024] | Series: Queer dharma library. | Includes bibliographical references.

Identifiers: LCCN: 2024926759 | ISBN: 9798896861478 (paperback 2nd edition) | 9798897787548 (audiobook 2nd edition)

Subjects: LCSH: Bodhicaryāvatāra. English. | Śāntideva, active 7th century. | Mahayana Buddhism--Doctrines--Poetry. | Buddhism--Doctrines--Poetry. | Bodhisattvas--Poetry. | Dharma (Buddhism) | Sexual minorities. | Gay people. | Spirituality. | Queer theology. | Queer theory. | Philosophy, Asian. | Identity (Psychology)--Religious aspects--Buddhism. | Homosexuality--Religious aspects--Buddhism. | Buddhist poetry. | BISAC: RELIGION / Buddhism / Tibetan. | RELIGION / Sexuality & Gender Studies. | SOCIAL SCIENCE / LGBTQ+ Studies.

Classification: LCC: BQ3142.E5 S63 2024 | DDC: 294.3/85--dc23

First published in 2024 by dFRAE Media Co. - Lexington, Kentucky

Library of Congress Control Number: 2024926759

Second edition

ISBN (paperback): 9798896861478
ISBN (hardcover): 9798895877869

ASIN (Kindle): B0DLR8WPV2

Part 1 and Part 3 are excerpted from "Compassion That Walk" by David Franklin Sparks. For more information, visit www.dfrae.net.

Cover art by Kristina Rambo

Contents

Preface   iv

I   The Prologue

OG Bodhisattva: The Story of Shantideva   3

II   The Clapback

1. The Benefit of the Awakened Spirit   23
2. Confessions: The Shade of it All   30
3. Embracing the Spirit of Awakening   38
4. Attending to That Enlightened State of Mind   41
5. Keeping Your Inner House in Check   47
6. The Enlightened Quality of Patience   59
7. The Enlightened Quality of Joyous Effort   73
8. The Enlightened Quality of Mindfulness   81
9. The Enlightened Quality of Wisdom   100
10. Dedication   117

III   The Aftermath

In Conclusion   127

About David Franklin Sparks   136

Contents

Preface

Darling readers,

When I first embarked on this fabulous journey of "Queering the Path to Enlightenment," my book series, I had one mission in mind: to serve Buddhist realness to our queer family in a language that speaks to our souls. Let's face it, honey - representation matters. For too long, our LGBTQ+ experiences have been sidelined in spiritual spaces, but the tea is, our unique perspectives bring a whole new flavor to understanding these ancient wisdom traditions.

It's like Buddhism and queerness were meant to be together - a perfect pairing, like a bold lip with a fierce contour. Both are about seeing beyond surface-level appearances, embracing authenticity, and cultivating compassion for all beings. And let's be real, many of us in the queer community have been pushed out of the churches and temples of our upbringing. We're spiritual seekers without a home, and baby, it's time we found our spiritual chosen family.

That's why I created this series, and why I'm serving up this full translation of Shantideva's "Way of the Bodhisattva." It's time we had access to these profound teachings in a voice that feels like home.

As you will read in Part 1, Shantideva was an 8th century Buddhist scholar who studied at Nalanda University. According to Tibetan legend, everyone at his university was sleeping on Shantideva– they thought he was giving major flop energy. His haters tried to put him on blast in front of the whole school, but Shantideva said 'bet' and delivered this absolutely iconic Buddhist wisdom that had everyone shook.

This is Shantideva's master class on the bodhisattva path. The Sanskrit title translates roughly to "Entering the Way of the Bodhisattva" and is known in English under various names including "Guide to the Bodhisattva's Way of Life" and "The Way of the Bodhisattva." In case you didn't know, a bodhisattva is shorter fancy term for a person who seeks awakening not just for themselves, but for the benefit of all.

The text was carried to Tibet where it was translated into Tibetan, and became a cornerstone of Buddhist study. Many English translations draw from both the Sanskrit original and its Tibetan rendering, along with centuries of commentary from Buddhist masters. This revered work serves as a practical guide for those aspiring to follow the way of the enlightened warrior.

I understood the original text by reading these translations:

- A Guide to the Bodhisattva Way of Life by Śāntideva, translated from the Sanskrit and Tibetan by Vesna A. Wallace and B. Alan Wallace. Snow Lion Publications, 1997.
- Bodhisattvācharyavatāra: Engaging in the Deeds of the Bodhisattva by Shantideva, translated by Toh See Gee, based on the earlier translations by Stephen Batchelor and others. Foundation for the Preservation of the Mahayana Tradition, 2007.

* * *

Now, let me spill some tea about how I approached this translation. I've gone verse by verse, honey, keeping the meaning intact while wrapping it in the fiercest queer vernacular. It's like we've taken Shantideva's timeless wisdom and dressed it up for the gala - still recognizable, but with added sparkle and sass.

For those commonly known Buddhist terms and names, I've kept them as is, with a little footnote realness to help you keep up. But for some of those obscure references that would have you googling for days? I've provided modern equivalents. Think less "obscure 1st-century sutra" and more "Pema Chödrön's latest bestseller."

Now, I won't lie to you - I faced some challenges. The original text sometimes serves some outdated perspectives, especially about women. But instead of sweeping it under the rug, I've addressed it head-on by keeping the essence of the message while translating it into advice that makes sense for our modern, inclusive world. So "don't teach women without a man present" becomes "know your boundaries and avoid situations that could read as sketchy." Same energy, less patriarchy.

What am I hoping to achieve with all this? Simple, darling. I want more of our queer siblings to discover the life-changing power of the dharma. I want you to find refuge in the three jewels and let compassion be your fiercest accessory as you strut down life's runway.

So whether you're a seasoned practitioner or a spiritual newbie, whether you're here for the Buddhist wisdom or just living for the queer flavor, know that you're welcome here. This is your space to explore, to question, to grow, and to shine.

Now, let's discover the bodhisattva within each of us. It's time to awaken, darlings - and look good doing it!

With all the love and sass in the universe,

David Franklin Sparks
Lexington, Kentucky

I

The Prologue

OG Bodhisattva: The Story of Shantideva

This book is a suppliment to the "Queering the Path to Enlightenment" series, which explores of Buddhist teachings through a contemporary queer lens. Book One introduces foundational Buddhist concepts and guides readers through the initial scope of the lamrim (stages of the path). Book Two delves deeper into the middle scope, examining how Buddhist masters like Shantideva revolutionized spiritual practice through radical acts of authenticity and courage. Through vivid accounts of legendary Buddhist figures - from the OG Buddha's journey of self-discovery to Milarepa's fierce transformation from black magic to enlightenment - the series illuminates how the path to awakening often parallels the queer experience of embracing one's true nature.

The following story of Shantideva, excerpted from Book Two: Compassion That Walk!, offers a taste of these powerful connections.

Picture it: 8th century India. The air is thick with incense, the streets are buzzing with spiritual seekers, and somewhere in the royal palace of Zahor in Gujarat, a baby boy is born who's about to change the game. This isn't just any baby - this is Shantideva, future Buddhist superstar and compassion icon.

Now, being born into royalty might sound like a dream come true - all the jewels, the fancy robes, the non-stop buffet of palace life. But for our boy Shantideva, it was like being stuck

4

in a glittery cage. From a young age, he was more interested in the sparkle of wisdom than the shine of his crown. Think of him as that kid who'd rather read philosophy books than attend their own Sweet Sixteen party - you know the type.

Legend has it that when Shantideva was just a wee prince, he had a dream that would make even the most far-out psychedelic trip look tame. In this dream, he found himself nibbling on some sort of mystical yogurt (yes, yogurt - the ancients were wild, darling). As he ate this divine dairy, who should appear but Manjushri, the Bodhisattva of Wisdom himself.

Picture Manjushri as the ultimate celestial queen - radiant, fierce, with a sword sharp enough to cut through illusion and a book of wisdom that makes Google look like a kindergarten primer. This fabulous apparition told Shantideva, "Child, if you want the real tea of existence, come find me. I'll be your spiritual GPS."

From that moment on, Shantideva was changed. It's like he got a glimpse behind the curtain of reality and realized that the royal show he was part of was just that - a show. He started seeing his princely duties as more of a drag than a privilege. While everyone else was living for the palace drama, our boy was in his room contemplating the nature of existence.

Fast forward to the night before Shantideva's coronation. The palace is in a tizzy, everyone's running around like it's five minutes before curtain call at a drag show. But where's the star of the show? Shantideva, in a move that would make any diva proud, has pulled the ultimate ghosting act. He's left the palace, his royal robes, and his crown behind, choosing instead to wrap himself in the simple robes of a monk.

Can you imagine the scandal? It's like if RuPaul decided to quit drag and become a hermit right before the Season 15 finale of Drag Race. The palace was shook, honey. But Shantideva wasn't just running away from something - he was running toward something bigger than any crown could offer.

After leaving the palace faster than your first girlfriend's cat when you tried to pet it, Shantideva headed straight for the Buddhist equivalent of an Ivy League education - Nalanda University. But this wasn't your typical campus experience. Nalanda was serving serious spiritual realness, with thousands of monks studying everything from logic to meditation, and debates fiercer than a vogue battle.

Now, here's where it gets interesting. Instead of announcing himself as ex-royalty (which would have been the ancient Indian equivalent of dropping "Do you know who my father is?"), our boy chose to keep it low-key. He became known as Bhusuku - literally "the one who just eats, sleeps, and strolls around."

Talk about a reputation! While other monks were out there showing off their philosophical chops like peacocks at a pride parade, Shantideva appeared to be doing absolutely nothing. The other monks were not having it. They were giving him more side-eye than a lesbian softball team gives to someone who showed up in heels.

So these shady monks decided to set up our boy for the ultimate public humiliation. They set up a high throne in the middle of the monastery and invited him to give a dharma talk. Their plan? Watch him stumble, fumble, and finally have an excuse to kick his royal tuchus out of Nalanda.

But honey, they didn't know who they were dealing with. They were not ready for what was about to go down. This was about to be the spiritual equivalent of Beyoncé dropping "Lemonade" - unexpected, mind-blowing, and about to change the game forever.

6

The day arrives, and the whole monastery shows up for what they think is going to be the academic equivalent of a train wreck. But Shantideva, channeling energy that would make even the most seasoned drag queen's highlight look dim, ascended that throne like he was climbing the stairs at the Met Gala. The crowd was all bets and giggles, waiting for the stumble. But our boy looks out at the sea of shady monks and asks, cool as a cucumber in a blizzard, "Would you like me to recite something familiar, or something new?"

The crowd, thinking they're so clever, calls for something new. And that's when Shantideva unleashes his magnum opus: "The Way of the Bodhisattva" (Bodhicaryavatara).

Picture it: The sun is high over Nalanda, the crowd is gagged, and Shantideva is just getting warmed up. He's flowing through chapter after chapter of pure spiritual wisdom, serving looks that could kill delusion and dropping truth bombs that would make even the shadiest monks stop and think.

But it's when he gets to Chapter 9 - the one about wisdom and emptiness - that things get really fierce. As he begins to explain the deepest nature of reality, our boy starts to rise from his throne. And not in a "let me stand up for emphasis" way - we're talking full-on levitation, floating higher and higher until he straight-up disappears into the sky.

Now that's what I call a mic drop.

The monks who had tried to read him were now reading his teachings instead, frantically trying to write down every word he'd spoken. Turns out our sleepy queen had been doing more than just eating and napping - he'd been composing this masterpiece in his head the whole time. It's like finding out that quiet kid in your drama club had secretly written, directed, and starred in their own one-person show that would revolutionize theater.

But here's the gag: Different groups of monks remembered different numbers of chapters. Some wrote down nine, others ten. They were running around like tops trying to figure out which version was correct. Finally, some monks traveled to find Shantideva (talk about a fan club!) and asked him directly. He confirmed there were ten chapters and helped them find the complete text.

What makes this story so important isn't just the magical elements (though honey, those are fierce). It's that Shantideva was teaching us something profound about authenticity and appearances. Here was someone who looked like a mess on the outside but was cultivating incredible wisdom on the inside. Sound familiar? It's like every queer person who ever had to hide their true self while developing their inner strength.

His masterpiece, "A Guide to the Bodhisattva's Way of Life," isn't just some dusty old text - it's a revolutionary manifesto about transforming yourself through compassion and wisdom. It's about seeing through the drama of everyday life to find something deeper and more meaningful. It's about being fierce in your dedication to helping others, even when nobody understands what you're doing.

Shantideva's work has been spilling the tea on spiritual transformation for over 1,200 years now. The Dalai Lama teaches from it regularly. It's been translated into more languages than Madonna has reinvented herself. And its message about combining wisdom with compassion is more relevant than ever.

Think about it: Here was someone who gave up every privilege, faced ridicule and shade, and still came through with more grace than a ballroom legend. Why? Because he understood that true happiness isn't about external validation - it's about transforming your mind and helping others.

The Relevance: Why Shantideva's Tea Still Hits Different

So why should we care about this ancient Indian prince-turned-monk in our modern queer lives? Because honey, Shantideva's story and teachings speak to us on levels deeper than your most introspective 3 AM Tumblr posts.

First off, let's talk about authenticity. Shantideva chose to live his truth even when it meant disappointing every single expectation his family and society had for him. Sound familiar? It's like coming out times ten - not just about your identity, but about your whole way of being in the world. He showed us that sometimes you have to let people think you're a mess while you're doing your inner work. (And isn't that just the perfect metaphor for those awkward years of questioning your gender or sexuality?)

Then there's his teachings about compassion. In "Guide to the Bodhisattva's Way of Life," he spills the tea about how to genuinely care for others without burning yourself out - something every queer activist needs to hear. He taught that real compassion comes from wisdom, not just emotional reaction. It's like understanding the difference between posting a rainbow flag during Pride month and actually showing up for trans youth all year round.

But perhaps his most radical teaching was about emptiness - the ultimate nature of reality. Now, before you roll your eyes

9

thinking this is some abstract philosophical nonsense, listen up: Shantideva was basically teaching that nothing exists in the solid, fixed way we think it does. Including gender. Including sexuality. Including all the boxes society tries to put us in.

When he talks about seeing through appearances to the deeper nature of reality, he's giving us tools to dismantle not just heteronormativity, but all the ways we get stuck in limiting beliefs about ourselves and others. It's like gender theory meets Buddhist philosophy, but make it practical.

So how do we work with Shantideva's teachings today? Start by approaching your own path with the same authenticity he showed. Maybe you're not ready to float away during a teaching, but you can be real about where you're at and what you're working on.

Take his teachings on patience when dealing with haters (and honey, he had some things to say about that). He taught that those who oppose us are actually helping us develop strength - like emotional resistance training. Next time someone's serving ignorance, remember you're getting a free workout for your compassion muscles.

And most importantly, remember his message about combining wisdom with compassion. In our community, we need both - the wisdom to see through societal conditioning and the compassion to help others who are still struggling with it.

Shantideva's story reminds us that sometimes the most revolutionary act is simply being true to your path, even when others don't understand it. He showed us that real transformation doesn't always look Instagram-worthy from the outside, and that's okay.

So the next time you're feeling misunderstood, or like your spiritual path is taking you in directions your friends don't get, remember our boy Shantideva. Remember that sometimes the ones they call lazy or weird or too much are the ones who end up changing the world.

After all, as Shantideva might say if he were here today: "Let them think what they want - you focus on developing that bodhisattva mind, queen."

* * *

Now, let's zoom in on that bodhichitta, because honey, it's the star of this show. Bodhichitta is like the ultimate queer superpower. It's the wish to attain enlightenment for the sake of all beings. Imagine if Lady Gaga decided she wanted to make everyone a superstar, not just herself. That's bodhichitta energy, darling.

Shantideva breaks bodhichitta down into two types: aspirational and engaged. Aspirational bodhichitta is like when you see that super fierce outfit and think, "I'm gonna werk that one day." It's the wish, the intention, the dream of enlightenment for all.

Engaged bodhichitta is when you actually start strutting down that spiritual runway. It's taking the vows, doing the practice, and living that bodhisattva life 24/7. It's like the difference between saying "I support the community" and actually showing up to protest for LGBTQ+ rights.

Now, you might be thinking, "Girl, that sounds like a lot of work." And you're not wrong. But Shantideva's got you covered with some serious motivation. He says cultivating bodhichitta

11

is like alchemy - it can transform your hot mess of a mind into pure spiritual gold.

In chapter one, he serves this truth tea: "Just as a flash of lightning on a dark, cloudy night for an instant brightly illuminates all, likewise in this world, through the power of Buddha, a wholesome thought rarely and briefly appears."

Translation? That moment of compassion you feel? It's rare and precious, like finding a vintage Valentino at a thrift store. Cherish it, work it, make it your signature look.

But Shantideva doesn't just leave us with pretty words. He gives us practical advice that's as applicable today as it was 1300 years ago. Take this gem from chapter six on patience:

"Why be unhappy about something if you can change it? And if you can't change it, why be unhappy about it?"

Honey, that's some advice that could save you years of therapy. It's like he's telling us, "Don't let the haters get you down, and don't be your own hater either."

And when it comes to dealing with enemies? Shantideva's got a take hotter than your latest Insta thirst trap. He says our enemies are actually our greatest teachers. They give us the opportunity to practice patience and compassion. It's like that queen who always tries to steal your spotlight - she's not your rival, she's your spiritual gym trainer, helping you buff up those compassion muscles.

But perhaps the most revolutionary part of "The Way of the Bodhisattva" is its teaching on emptiness. No, not the emptiness you feel after scrolling through your ex's Instagram. We're talking about the ultimate nature of reality.

Shantideva says everything is empty of inherent existence. It's like realizing that the labels we put on ourselves - gay, straight, bi, trans, queer - are just concepts. They're useful, sure, like a good pair of shapewear, but they're not the essence of who we are.

This understanding of emptiness is the key to true compassion. When we realize we're all just swirling clouds of causes and conditions, with no solid core, it becomes easier to feel connected to everyone. It's like realizing that under all the makeup, wigs, and padding, we're all just humans trying to slay this thing called life.

Now, I know what you're thinking. "This all sounds great, but how do I actually do this in my daily life?" Well, fear not, because Shantideva's got practical tips that are more useful than a drag queen's wig glue.

For example, he advises us to practice tonglen - a meditation where you breathe in the suffering of others and breathe out happiness to them. It's like being a spiritual air purifier, honey. You're taking in all the negativity and drama, transforming it with your fabulous compassion, and sending out nothing but good vibes.

He also emphasizes the importance of rejoicing in the good fortune of others. See someone else succeeding? Instead of being shady, celebrate them! It's like cheering for another queen when she turns a killer look. Their success doesn't dim your spotlight - if anything, it makes the whole stage brighter.

Shantideva's teachings remind us that being a bodhisattva isn't about being perfect. It's about striving, about picking yourself up every time you fall off those spiritual stilettos. He says, "If you can, you should always provide help and happiness to all. If you can't, you should at least not harm anyone." It's like spiritual harm reduction, darling. Do what you can, where you are, with what you've got.

The beauty of Shantideva's work is that it speaks to everyone, from the spiritual newbie to the enlightenment elder. It's like a spiritual department store - there's something here for everyone, whether you're shopping in basics or haute couture.

For our queer family, Shantideva's teachings offer a powerful framework for navigating a world that's not always kind to us. His emphasis on patience and compassion gives us tools to deal with discrimination and hate. His teachings on emptiness remind us that the labels society tries to put on us don't define our worth.

Moreover, the bodhisattva path resonates deeply with the queer experience. Many of us know what it's like to suffer because of who we are. We understand the importance of building chosen families and communities. In many ways, we're already practicing the bodhisattva path - now we're just adding some spiritual glitter to it.

Let's dive deeper into how Shantideva's teachings can apply to our fabulous queer lives:

Compassion for Ourselves: Shantideva teaches us to cultivate compassion for all beings, and honey, that includes ourselves. In a world that often tells us we're wrong or broken, practicing self-compassion is a radical act. It's like being your own fairy godmother, waving that wand of kindness over your own heart.

Patience with Our Journey: Coming out, transitioning, finding our place in the community - these processes take time. Shantideva's teachings on patience remind us that it's okay to take things one fabulous step at a time. Your journey is your own, and it's not a race.

Enthusiasm for Activism: Shantideva's chapter on enthusiasm can fuel our fight for equality. It's a reminder that every small action counts, whether it's attending a Pride parade or having a heartfelt conversation with a family member who doesn't understand.

Wisdom in Identity: The teachings on emptiness can help us navigate the complex world of gender and sexuality. Labels can be useful tools, but they're not the totality of who we are. We're as fluid and boundless as the cosmos itself, darling.

Generosity in Community: Shantideva emphasizes the importance of giving. In our community, this can manifest as mentoring younger LGBTQ+ folks, volunteering at queer organizations, or simply being there for a friend in need.

Ethical Living in a Complex World: The bodhisattva vows give us a framework for ethical living that goes beyond societal norms. It's about doing what's truly kind and beneficial, not just what's expected.

Meditation for Mental Health: In a community that faces higher rates of anxiety and depression, Shantideva's teachings on meditation offer valuable tools for mental wellbeing. It's like a spa day for your mind, honey.

Transforming Discrimination: Shantideva teaches us to transform adverse circumstances into the path. This means we can use experiences of discrimination as opportunities to cultivate compassion and work towards change.

Interconnectedness in Diversity: The concept of emptiness teaches us that we're all interconnected. In the diverse spectrum of our community, this reminds us that our liberation is bound up with everyone else's.

Dedication of Merit: By dedicating the merit of our actions to all beings, we expand our impact beyond ourselves. Every time we stand up for our rights, we're standing up for everyone's rights.

Shantideva's legacy continues to sparkle through the centuries. His words have inspired countless practitioners, from the Dalai Lama to Western Buddhist teachers. It's like his wisdom is the little black dress of Buddhism - timeless, versatile, and always in style.

The Dalai Lama, in particular, is a huge fan. He's said that he recites verses from "The Way of the Bodhisattva" every day. Imagine that - the spiritual leader of Tibetan Buddhism, starting his day with Shantideva's words. It's like he's putting on his spiritual armor before facing the world. If it's good enough for the Dalai Lama, honey, you know it's got to be fierce.

But it's not just the big names in Buddhism who are feeling Shantideva's vibe. His teachings have sashayed their way into Western Buddhism too. Teachers like Pema Chödrön have taken Shantideva's words and made them accessible to modern audiences. It's like they've taken this ancient wisdom and given it a contemporary makeover - still classic, but with a fresh twist.

Pema Chödrön, in her book "Start Where You Are," uses Shantideva's teachings as a foundation for dealing with the messiness of everyday life. She's like the cool aunt of Buddhism, taking Shantideva's high philosophy and turning it into practical advice for dealing with your annoying coworker or your own inner critic.

Even in the world of pop psychology, you can see Shantideva's influence. All those self-help books talking about the power of compassion and mindfulness? Honey, Shantideva was serving that wisdom centuries ago. He was ahead of his time, like a fashion designer whose runway looks don't hit the streets for decades.

Now, let's talk about how Shantideva's teachings can help us navigate some of the unique challenges our queer community faces:

Dealing with Homophobia and Transphobia: Shantideva's teachings on patience and compassion give us tools to deal with discrimination without losing our fabulous selves in the process. It's like having an emotional shield that deflects hate while radiating fabulousness.

Coming Out: The bodhisattva path is all about authenticity and courage. Sound familiar? Coming out is a bodhisattva move, honey. You're not just being true to yourself, you're helping create a more accepting world for others.

Body Image Issues: In a community that often places a high value on physical appearance, Shantideva's teachings on the nature of reality can be liberating. Your body is just your current outfit, darling. Your true self is so much more fabulous and expansive.

Chosen Family Dynamics: Shantideva's emphasis on compassion and patience can help us navigate the complex relation-

17

ships in our chosen families. It's like having a guidebook for building and maintaining your queer support network.

Activism Burnout: The bodhisattva path is a marathon, not a sprint. Shantideva's teachings can help us stay committed to the fight for equality while also taking care of ourselves. It's like learning how to be a diva on stage and a zen master backstage.

Dating and Relationships: Emptiness teachings can liberate us from unrealistic expectations in relationships. Plus, Shantideva's advice on patience and compassion? Relationship gold, honey.

Intersectionality: Shantideva's vision of universal compassion aligns beautifully with intersectional approaches to LGBTQ+ activism. It's about lifting everyone up, not just those who look or love like us.

HIV/AIDS and Health: For a community that's been deeply impacted by the HIV/AIDS crisis, Shantideva's teachings on impermanence and the preciousness of human life can be particularly poignant. It's a reminder to live fully and love fiercely, no matter what.

Queer Joy: Sometimes, in the face of challenges, we forget to celebrate our fabulousness. Shantideva's teachings on rejoicing remind us to revel in the beauty of our community and our individual journeys.

Spiritual Reconciliation: For those of us who've felt rejected by traditional religions, Shantideva offers a spiritual path that celebrates compassion and authenticity. It's like finding a spiritual home that loves you exactly as you are.

As we wrap up this deep dive into Shantideva's world, let's take a moment to appreciate the fabulousness of this spiritual journey we're on. Shantideva shows us that being spiritual doesn't mean being somber or boring. It's about living life fully, loving fiercely, and serving compassion realness every day.

Remember, darlings, in the words of Shantideva himself: "For as long as space endures and for as long as living beings remain, until then may I too abide to dispel the misery of the world." It's like he's encouraging us to be the glitter in the darkness, the rainbow after the storm.

So, my beautiful queer family, are you ready to walk the bodhisattva path? Are you prepared to turn your compassion up to eleven and your ego down to zero? Remember, in the immortal words of Shantideva (as interpreted by your truly): "If you can love yourself and everyone else, honey, you're already halfway to enlightenment."

Now go forth, my fabulous bodhisattvas-in-training. May your compassion be as fierce as your contour, your wisdom as sharp as your winged eyeliner, and your bodhichitta as expansive as a drag queen's wig collection. The cosmic runway awaits, and you're about to slay it with kindness!

In the grand show of life, we're all here to help each other shine. So spread that bodhichitta like it's glitter, and let's make this world a more fabulous place for everyone. Shantideva would be proud, darling.

II

The Clapback

1. The Benefit of the Awakened Spirit

1. Serving nothing but respect to all the fully realized Buddhas who've come before, their legendary children, and everyone else worthy of a crown, I'm about to break down the essential guide for how to werk it like a spiritual boss. No shade, just facts from the ancient texts.
2. Look, I'm not claiming to spill any new tea here, and I'm no literary diva. Truth is, I'm not even doing this for anybody else - I'm just translating this to get my own mind seasoned.
3. But doing this makes my faith feel extra fierce, and who knows? Maybe somebody else out there with a mind like mine might find it useful too.
4. This fabulous human life we've got? With all its privileges and possibilities? Harder to come by than a vintage Valentino. If you don't werk it while you've got it, when will you get another chance?
5. Let me put it this way: a dark and stormy night, then BAM! - lightning flashes and everything's clear for a hot second. That's what it's like when the Buddha's influence hits - suddenly folks get that spiritual clarity, even if it's just for

a moment. Tibetans call it bodhicitta.[1]

6. That's why being virtuous is usually about as stable as a baby queen in six-inch heels, while negative energy comes through stronger than a power ballad. Without this enlightened state of mind, what else could possibly stand up to all that drama?

7. The spiritual legends, who have been featuring this for centuries, all say that an awakened spirit is the ultimate blessing - it easily increases joy and benefits countless others.

8. So look, if you're over all the suffering this world is serving, if you want to help others stop struggling, and if you're ready to experience more joy, then don't even think about giving up on this enlightened state of mind.

9. The moment this fierce spiritual energy awakens in you? Baby, you go from basic to blessed. Even if you were a complete mess before, suddenly you're spiritual royalty - we're talking respect from both humans and deities, okurrr?

10. It's like the ultimate makeover for your dusty old consciousness - turning that basic mindset into pure spiritual diamonds. So hold onto this transformative energy like it's the last tube of your favorite cosmetic, and the company has gone out of business.

11. The most legendary spiritual victors, whose minds are deeper than the ocean, have checked this out thoroughly. So if you're trying to sashay away from all this worldly

---

[1] Bodhicitta: The "awakened mind" or "mind of enlightenment." The altruistic intention to attain enlightenment for the benefit of all beings. In Mahayana Buddhism, it's considered the foundation of the bodhisattva path.

drama, grab onto this enlightened mindset like your life depends on it.

12. Most virtues[2] are like one-hit wonders. They have their moment and then fade like cheap hair dye. But this enlightened attitude? It's more like Betty White's career - it just keeps producing fruit and gets better with time.

13. The spirit of awakening is like having the fiercest security team. Even if you've done some seriously questionable things, you can overcome those fears real quick. Why aren't more people getting their life from this?

14. This energy burns away negative karma[3] faster than a dramatic social-media callout destroys a reputation. Just ask Maitreya[4] - she was spilling this tea to Sudhana[5] about all the incredible benefits[6].

15. This enlightened mindset comes in two flavors - the "I want to" and the "I'm actually doing it." Laying in bed,

---

[2] Positive qualities and actions that lead to beneficial results and spiritual progress. In Buddhism, these include generosity, ethics, patience, diligence, concentration, and wisdom.

[3] Karma: The law of cause and effect in Buddhism, where actions create corresponding results. Positive actions create positive results, negative actions create suffering.

[4] Maitreya: Often depicted seated with legs down, ready to rise. Associated with loving-kindness and the next golden age of Buddhist teachings. Believed by some to reappear on Earth.

[5] Sudhanna: Protagonist in the Gandavyuha Sutra. A youth who embarks on a spiritual journey, meeting 53 teachers. Symbolizes the bodhisattva's quest for enlightenment.

[6] In the Gandavyuhasutra (Array of Stalks Sutra), Maitreya explains to Sudhana how the mind of enlightenment is like a seed, a field, the earth, and various powerful objects, emphasizing its transformative and protective qualities.

Aspiring-Mind be like: "I should go to the club." The mind can visualize it, but the body's still under the covers. Strutting down the street, heels clicking, Engaging-Mind be like: "I should touch up my mug before I get to the club." The mind and body are both in on the action.

16. In bodhicitta terms: Aspiring-Bodhicitta: You're all about that enlightenment and helping others, but you're not necessarily practicing the six perfections[7] yet. Engaging-Bodhicitta: You're out there slaying those six perfections, actively working towards enlightenment and serving the community. It's like the difference between one who yearns to travel, and a traveler. It's the traveler who easily clocks the difference between them.

17. The engaging mind is produced by the wishing mind. Both are valuable and powerful. But actually doing the work? Child, that's a whole other level of spiritual fierceness.

18. From the moment an Engaging-Mind makes the determination to develop the enlightened qualities of the Awakened-Mind,

19. From that exact moment, honey, even when you're sleeping or scrolling through TikTok, you're generating more good karma than there is space in the sky.

20. And this isn't just me talking - the Buddha himself spilled this tea in the Subahuprccha[8] for all those folks still playing in the spiritual kiddie pool.

---

[7] Six perfections: generosity, ethics, patience, joyous effort, concentration, and wisdom. Enlightened qualities, also known as far reaching attitudes, to be perfected before one can attain liberation.

[8] Subahuprccha: A sutra in which the Buddha answers questions from the bodhisattva Subahu about various aspects of the bodhisattva path and practices

21. No shade. A well-intentioned person who thinks "I'm gonna help people access mental health resources" - just that thought alone creates more merit than a perfect score from all the judges.

22. So imagine the karma you're serving when you're ready to snatch away ALL the suffering from EVERY single being and give them nothing but pure joy? Now that's what I call a generous queen!

23. Let's be real - even your most supportive mother/father/-parent doesn't serve that level of altruism. And the gods? The sages? Even RuPaul? None of them are giving you this kind of unconditional love for all beings.

24. If these beings never even dreamed of wanting this kind of happiness for themselves, what makes you think they'd want it for others? That's like expecting someone who's never seen "Paris Is Burning" to understand reading.

25. This kind of selfless love? It's completely unprecedented, darling. It's like the first Pride parade, the first voguing competition - something completely new and revolutionary that changes everything.

26. How can you even measure the good karma of this mindset? It's like trying to count the sequins on Liberace's entire wardrobe - it's the seed of all joy and the cure for all drama.

27. If just wanting to help others already gets more respect than a perfect runway walk, imagine what actually working for everyone's complete happiness gets you!

28. These poor confused queens out here - running away from suffering but heading right for it, like wearing six-inch heels to a marathon. Thinking they're chasing happiness but destroying it faster than a slot machine.

29. But this enlightened mindset? It's serving pure joy to everyone who's starving for happiness, and snatching away all the sorrows from those who are struggling. Now that's what I call a legendary humanitarian queer!

30. It clears away all confusion like the best makeup remover. Tell me, where else are you gonna find this kind of saint? This kind of friend? This level of merit?

31. People get praised just for returning a favor - giving back what they got. So what do we say about these spiritual queens who are out here serving kindness that nobody even asked for?

32. If someone gets called virtuous for throwing a few coins to a couple of people, or serving lunch at the shelter once in a blue moon...

33. Then what about these legendary beings who are promising to fulfill EVERYONE'S wishes - like, ALL beings, until the end of time? That's more generous than a rich gay uncle with no kids!

34. Here's the tea the Buddha spilled: if you throw shade at one of these enlightened divas, you're going to be dealing with that bad karma for more lifetimes than you have social-media followers.

35. But if you're giving them nothing but love? Baby, the good karma comes flooding in faster than likes on a thirst trap. Even if someone comes for them hard, these queens just naturally respond with more kindness than a supportive mother.

36. So I'm bowing down to everyone who's developed this precious enlightened mindset. I'm running to these fountains of joy for refuge. Even when you mess up with them, they turn it into a blessing - now that's what I call

unbothered!

2. Confessions: The Shade of it All

1. To get this precious enlightened mindset, I'm laying out the most fabulous offerings to the fully realized queens who came before, to their flawless teachings, and to their spiritual children who are serving nothing but excellence.
2. I'm offering EVERYTHING, honey -
3. every flower that's blooming, every crystal that's glowing, all the fresh mountain springs, those gorgeous forest hideaways, every vine dripping with blossoms, trees heavy with fruit,
4. all the designer perfumes of the gods, those lakes covered in lotus realness, sacred geese serving vocals,
5. everything growing wild and everything cultivated - all of it, extending through all of space!
6. I'm visualizing all of this and offering it to the ultimate spiritual divas and their children. May these queens who deserve nothing but the best, who live for showing compassion to little old me, accept my offerings!
7. Look, I know I'm serving zero merit realness right now - I'm basically spiritual broke. But these protective queens live to help others, so maybe they'll use their power to accept my humble offerings anyway?

8. I'm offering my whole self to these enlightened legends and their legendary children. Accept me, supreme beings! I'm yours to serve!

9. Under your protection, I won't have to fear this messy cycle of existence anymore. I'm ready to help all beings, leave my problematic past behind, and stop creating more drama!

10. I'm creating these crystalline bathhouses, honey - we're talking jeweled pillars, pearl canopies, floors so clear you could check your makeup in them.

11. And I'm bathing all these enlightened beings in sacred water, sprinkling flowers everywhere, playing the most heavenly music.

12. Then I'm drying them off with the softest, most fragrant towels and dressing them in garments that would make Billy Porter gag!

13. I'm adorning all these spiritual icons - Samantabhadra[9], Ajita[10], Manjughosa[11], Lokesvara[12] - like they're heading to the Met Gala.

14. We're talking divine fabrics, precious jewels, and perfumes

---

[9] Samantabhadra: prominent bodhisattva, often associated with practice, meditation, and the essence of all Buddha's conduct; embodies the power of wisdom, meditation, and the practice of vows; Often depicted riding a white elephant with six tusks, symbolizing the perfection of the six transcendent virtues.

[10] Ajita: Another name for Maitreya, the future Buddha. Means "Unconquered" or "Invincible."

[11] Manjughosa: Bodhisattva of wisdom. Depicted as a youth with a sword cutting through ignorance. Associated with insight and eloquence.

[12] Lokesvara: Another name for Avalokiteshvara, the bodhisattva of compassion. Means "Lord of the World."

so strong they could fill a thousand million worlds. Their bodies are glowing like perfectly polished gold - that's the kind of shine we're serving!

15. The flowers I'm offering? More stunning than any Pride parade float - mandaravas[13], blue lotuses, everything arranged like it's for a royal wedding.

16. The incense is giving celestial realness, and the feast I'm laying out would make any episode of "Queer Eye" look basic.

17. And those jeweled lamps on golden lotus stands? Child, the lighting is PERFECT.

18. For these beings who are nothing but love, I'm manifesting palaces that would make Versace clutch his pearls - we're talking pearl garlands, jewel ornaments, songs of praise filling every corner.

19. And those parasols? Golden handles, inlaid with pearls, raised to perfection - giving more elegance than a ballroom legend!

20. Let these offerings rise up like the most fabulous cloud formation you've ever seen! Let there be music that makes everyone feel their fantasy!

21. And may jewels and flowers rain down on all the holy objects like nature's own pride confetti!

22. Just like Manjughosa and crew serve praise to the enlightened few, I'm giving these protectors my praise too,

23. Their virtues deeper than ocean blue! Let my verses rise and soar through the air, Like harmonious clouds without compare!

---

[13] The mandārava (coral tree) flower, considered a divine flower in Buddhist tradition often used as offerings to Buddhas and celestial beings.

32

24. To every Buddha throughout space and time, Their teachings and community so fine,
25. I'm bowing down with all my heart - Every atom of me taking part! To their shrines and resting spaces too,
26. To every teacher tried and true,
27. I'm seeking refuge, pure and bright, Till I reach that enlightened height!
28. With hands clasped tight, I'm asking please, All you Buddhas, hear my pleas!
29. All the mess that I've created, All the drama I've generated, Every shady thing I've celebrated, Every sin I've instigated
30. From lives beyond all counting still, I'm spilling all this bitter pill
31. Whatever shade I might have thrown at the Three Jewels[14] upon their throne, at parents, teachers, everyone - All that mess that I have done, with body, speech, or messy mind, I'm leaving all that trash behind!
32. Yes I have faults, I'm saying true, But I'm confessing them too
33. How will I escape all this? Before my karma comes to claim me?
34. Death doesn't care if you're ready or not, Whether you're sick or whether you're fine. It comes like lightning at the club - and often without warning signs.
35. I've caused all this drama, that's true, for friends and enemies alike. Never thinking I'd have to leave them all behind.

---

[14] Three Jewels: The Buddha (the enlightened teacher), the Dharma (the teachings), and the Sangha (the spiritual community). The core objects of refuge in Buddhism

33

36. My enemies won't stick around. My friends will fade away. Nothing's gonna last forever, that's all I can say.

37. Life's like a dream you had - especially the good ones. Once it's gone, it's gone for good.

38. Even now I've watched them pass - Friends and foes, they disappear. But all that karma that we created? That's still right here.

39. I forgot how fast this life goes by, Lost in delusion's haze. Between my loving and my hating, I've wasted all these days.

40. My life's tick-tocking down for real, Each minute slipping past. You think death's gonna skip me? No, none of us will last.

41. When I'm lying on my deathbed, even with my family near, the truth is that I'll face that final moment all alone, my dear.

42. When death's bouncers come to get you, no friend can help you stay. Only good karma is your backstage pass, and I ain't worked on that today.

43. Oh honey, I was clueless, About this dangerous game. Chasing after temporary pleasures, Living for the fame.

44. They take you to the doctor's office, Cut you open wide. Parched and scared, you see the world From the losing side.

45. Death's messengers sashay in, serving terror realness while I'm a hot mess express, fear-fever and all.

46. Eyes darting like it's last call at the club, I'm desperate for a spiritual bodyguard. Any takers?

47. No shelter in sight, I'm back to square one confusion. What's a queen to do in this fear-fest?

48. Jinas[15], I'm running to you now. Your protection is the hottest ticket in town.
49. Dharma[16], you fabulous fear-slayer, I'm all in. And don't forget the Bodhisattva[17] squad - I need all the help I can get.
50. Shaking like a leaf, I'm offering myself to Samantabhadra and Manjughosa. Take the wheel, honeys!
51. Avalokita[18], compassion personified, hear my cry! This sinner needs your fiercest protection.
52. Akasagarbha[19], Ksitigarbha[20], all you merciful divas - I'm calling your names like it's roll call at the pearly gates.

---

[15] Jina: Sanskrit for "victor" or "conqueror." An honorific title for the Buddha and other enlightened beings who have overcome all mental afflictions and achieved spiritual liberation.

[16] Dharma: The Buddha's teachings and commentary thereof; also means "truth" or "reality." Can refer to both spiritual teachings and all phenomena.

[17] Bodhisattva: One who seeks enlightenment for the benefit of all beings. Embodies compassion and wisdom, vowing to liberate others before attaining full Buddhahood.

[18] Avalokita: revered bodhisattva, embodying infinite compassion.; Often depicted with multiple arms and heads to represent their ability to help all beings simultaneously. In Tibet, known as Chenrezig and associated with the Dalai Lama. In East Asia, frequently portrayed in female form as Guanyin; Known for the vow to hear and respond to the cries of all sentient beings.

[19] Akasagarbha: bodhisattva, associated with boundless wisdom and memory; Often paired with Ksitigarbha as one of the Eight Great Bodhisattvas; Believed to possess infinite knowledge, like space containing all phenomena.

[20] Ksitigarbha: bodhisattva, often depicted as a monk with a staff and wish-fulfilling jewel; Known for the vow to not achieve Buddhahood until all hells are emptied; Associated with the liberation of beings in lower realms, protection of travelers and children, and as a guide for the deceased.

53. Vajri[21], even Death's crew runs screaming when you show up. I'm bowing down, faster than you can say "slay."

54. I ghosted your advice before, but now I'm back, fear nipping at my Louboutins. Help a sister out, and make it snappy!

55. We run to the doc for a sniffle, but ignore the cure for life's entire messy playlist? Make it make sense.

56. One bug can clear out a continent, no tea or shade can fix it. Yet we're out here ignoring the cosmic cure-all.

57. Brushing off the Awakened Healer? Shame on me, delusion's poster child.

58. We tiptoe on pebbles but dance on the edge of forever. The irony is not lost on this fool.

59. Thinking death's not on today's agenda? Honey, it's more certain than a diva's encore.

60. Who's handing out immortality passes? This borrowed time's slipping away faster than discount designer.

61. Past thrills are fading like last year's highlights. Was ignoring wisdom worth this lackluster afterparty?

62. When I ghost this mortal coil, friends and foes alike get left on read. What's the point of all this drama?

63. Day and night, one thought's on repeat: how to dodge the karmic debt collector when the bill comes due?

64. Every slip-up, every messy moment, every rule I bent 'til it snapped - I've been hoarding them like they're going out of style.

65. Shook to the core, I'm laying it all out for the Protectors.

---

[21] Vajri: Often depicted as a wrathful deity holding a vajra (thunderbolt scepter); Associated with power, protection, and the swift destruction of obstacles on the spiritual path.

Hands clasped, bowing 'til my ego breaks.

66. Cosmic guides, witness my hot mess express. Let this confession be my first step towards less mess, more blessed.

3. Embracing the Spirit of Awakening

1. I'm living for all the good vibes out there! It's like watching the finale of the best reality show out there - nothing but joy! May all those messy queens find their moment to shine!
2. I'm gagging over beings breaking free from their cycles of drama. And let's hear it for those legendary children reaching enlightenment - werk!
3. These spiritual queens and kings are serving awakening realness, and I'm eating it up like it's the last slice of rainbow cake!
4. I'm on my knees, hands clasped, begging these enlightened beings to light up the path for all the confused kittens out there stumbling in the dark.
5. Listen up, you fabulous Buddhas! Don't you dare sashay away to Nirvana[22] just yet. We need you here, keeping it lit for eons to come!
6. All this good karma I'm serving up? May it snatch away

---

[22] Nirvana: The ultimate state of enlightenment in Buddhism; literally means "blowing out" or "extinction." Refers to the end of all suffering and the cycle of rebirth through the complete elimination of all mental afflictions and desires.

everyone's suffering faster than a lesbian's u-haul on moving day.

7. Call me Dr. Fabulous, 'cause I'm here to cure what ails ya! I'll be your nurse, your emotional support, whatever you need until you're serving nothing but healthy realness.

8. I'm raining down snacks and drinks like it's happy hour at the hottest inclusive bar in town. No more hunger and thirst in this house!

9. For all you broke boys out there, I'm your sugar daddy now. Whatever you need, I got you covered like the perfect setting spray.

10. Honey, I'm giving it all away - my body, my stuff, all my good deeds. It's like the biggest charity show you've ever seen, and everyone's invited!

11. Giving it all up? That's the ultimate self-actualization, darling. And if I gotta let it all go, might as well share it with the family.

12. I'm offering up this body for the greater good. Beat it, paint it, throw shade at it - do what you gotta do. I'm unbothered.

13. Use me, laugh at me, make me your slave - I don't care!

14. I'm here to serve, and I'm serving it with a smile.

15. Even if you come at me with more drama than a processing circle, I hope you get everything you want.

16. Yes, even you haters - may you find your way to enlightenment too!

17. Need a protector? A guide? A bridge? Honey, I'm your all-in-one spiritual Swiss Army knife.

18. Whatever you need, I'm here to provide.

19. I'm your wish-fulfilling gem, your lucky charm, your power mantra, and your miracle cure. I'm the tree of

life and the cow of abundance all rolled into one!

20. Just like Mother Earth is here for all of us, I'm gonna be here for every queer, every ally,

21. and every confused kitten out there until we're all free and liberated.

22. Those legendary enlightened ones who came before? I'm following in their footsteps.

23. Time for me to werk it and spread that awakening love!

24. Now that I've embraced my inner spiritual diva, I'm gonna nurture it like it's my chosen children on their first night out.

25. Honey, my life just got its glow-up! I've been reborn into the house of Buddha, and I'm ready to serve some enlightened realness.

26. Everything I do now will be on brand with this Buddha family.

27. It's like I found a designer necklace at a thrift store - this awakening spirit just popped up out of nowhere!

28. This spirit of awakening? It's the ultimate life hack.

29. It's the cure for what ails ya, the shade for your spiritual thirst.

30. It's the contour for your karmic cheekbones. the empowerment for your activist soul.

31. It's dispelling ignorance faster than Mariah Carey dispels knowing Jennifer Lopez,

32. and even faster than a group text gets heated, over brunch plans.

33. Today, I'm inviting everyone to the ultimate spiritual ball. Gods, demons, humans - everyone's on the guest list. Let's celebrate in front of all this enlightened royalty!

4. Attending to That Enlightened State of Mind

1. Once you've committed to this enlightened mindset, honey, you better stay vigilant like it's the last sale at Barneys - no slacking on your spiritual training[23].

2. Even after making a commitment, it's totally valid to check yourself before you wreck yourself - especially if you jumped in without thinking it through.

3. But if something's been thoroughly examined by the most enlightened beings ever, their spiritual children, and little old me doing my absolute best - why would I toss that wisdom away like last night's leftovers?

4. If I make this sacred promise and then ghost everyone, after deceiving all these precious beings, what kind of mess am I manifesting for myself?

5. They say if you just promise to give away a bobby pin and

---

[23] Spiritual training: Buddhist term "bhāvanā," referring to mental cultivation and development through systematic practice. Includes meditation, study, and ethical conduct.

don't follow through, you end up as a hungry ghost[24] - and that's not the kind of haunting we're going for.

6. So imagine the karma when you publicly promise to bring supreme happiness to literally everyone in existence and then pull a vanishing act? The layers of that catastrophe, sweetie!

7. Only someone who sees absolutely everything could possibly understand how some folks still get liberated even after dropping their commitment to enlightenment like a hot potato.

8. For someone on this spiritual path, dropping the enlightened mindset is the biggest mistake you can make - like deleting your entire spiritual Instagram before backing it up, because it ruins everyone else's chance at happiness.

9. If blocking someone's virtue for even a hot second creates endless suffering because you've messed with their journey, imagine the karma of ruining it completely.

10. Destroy one being's happiness and you're already in hot water - now multiply that drama by every being in existence, sweetie. The math isn't mathing.

11. Between these major slip-ups and the power of this enlightened mindset, no wonder we keep spinning in circles like it's amateur night at the club.

12. So I better work this commitment like it's my last chance, because if I don't make the effort now, things are only going to get messier than a breakup at brunch.

13. Countless enlightened beings have been searching for

---

[24] Hungry ghost: One of the six realms of existence in Buddhist cosmology. Beings in this realm suffer from insatiable hunger and thirst, symbolizing the effects of greed and attachment.

every single one of us, but because of my own issues, I've been acting like I don't see their texts.

14. If I keep serving this energy, all I'm gonna get is more suffering - we're talking illness, death, dismemberment, and destruction. Not the aesthetic we're going for.

15. When will I get another perfect storm of opportunities like this - an enlightened teacher, actual faith, this human body, and the ability to create good karma? The odds are not in our favor, honey.

16. Health, food, and relatively low drama? This moment is more fleeting than a summer fling, and this body's basically a rental with no deposit.

17. The way I'm acting? The chances of getting another human life are slimmer than finding size 13 Louboutins at a sample sale.

18. If I can't even create good karma when everything's perfectly aligned, what makes me think I'll manage when I'm overwhelmed by lower realm realness[25]?

19. When you're not creating any good karma but piling up the bad, you won't even hear the words "good rebirth" for millions of lifetimes - and that's not a hyperbole.

20. That's why the enlightened one said getting a human life is about as likely as a turtle in the cosmic ocean popping its head through a tiny floating ring. The chances? Not great, sweetie.

21. One moment of bad karma can land you in the worst hell realm for an entire eon. So what are your chances of a

---

[25] Lower realm realness: References the three lower realms of existence in Buddhist cosmology: hell beings, hungry ghosts, and animals. These realms are considered particularly difficult for spiritual practice.

good rebirth when you've been collecting bad karma since before time was time?

22. After experiencing that hellscape, you're still not free. And while you're there? You just keep creating more bad karma - it's the most toxic relationship ever.

23. If I see all this and still can't get it together because I'm too busy scrolling through life, the guardians of hell are gonna read me for filth for a very long time.

24. That hell fire's gonna scorch this body for ages, and then the flames of regret are gonna make that burning seem like a warm summer breeze.

25. Somehow I lucked into this incredible opportunity that's harder to get than front row at Fashion Week, and even though I know this, I'm still setting myself up for hell realness.

26. It's like somebody put a spell on me. Who's doing this? Who's living in my mind rent-free making these choices?

27. These inner enemies - craving and hatred - don't even have physical form. They're not brave or smart. So why am I letting them run my life like they're my manager?

28. They've set up shop in my mind, causing chaos while living their best life, and I'm just... accepting it? The lack of boundaries is shocking.

29. If every human and celestial being came for me, even they couldn't throw me into the worst hell realm.

30. But these mental afflictions[26]? They'll toss me in there faster than you can say "bad life choices."

---

[26] Mental afflictions: Disturbing emotions and mental states that cloud the mind and cause suffering, such as anger, attachment, and ignorance. Considered the root causes of cyclic existence.

31. Regular enemies might stick around for a minute, but these mental afflictions? They've been here since the beginning and they're not planning their retirement.

32. Try to please regular enemies, and they might soften up. But the more you feed these mental afflictions, the more they make you suffer - like giving attention to toxic friends.

33. How can I feel fabulous about this cycle of existence when these eternal enemies are just chilling in my heart, causing all kinds of chaos?

34. How can I live my best life when these prison guards of cyclic existence, these absolute destroyers, are camping out in my heart's living room?

35. That's why I'm not backing down until these enemies are destroyed right in front of me. Even someone who gets mad about the smallest shade won't sleep until they've dealt with it.

36. In the middle of battle, warriors covered in wounds don't retreat without achieving their goal, even though they're fighting beings already destined for suffering and death.

37. So why should I get tired or depressed when I'm trying to destroy these natural enemies that cause all misery? Even if life throws a hundred obstacles my way, why should I give up?

38. If warriors wear their battle scars like accessories for no good reason, why should suffering bother me when I'm working toward the most magnificent goal in existence?

39. If people who fish, farm, or work the streets can handle whatever the weather serves them just to make a living, why can't I handle some difficulty for the sake of the entire world?

40. I promised to free every single being everywhere from

45

their mental afflictions, and here I am, still wrestling with my own - the irony isn't lost on me.

41. I was feeling my fantasy when I made those promises, not knowing my own limitations. But that doesn't mean I'm backing down from destroying these afflictions.

42. I'm staying focused on this mission, fixed on revenge - I'll fight every mental affliction except the ones that help eliminate other mental afflictions, because even a shady queen can be useful sometimes.

43. Let my insides spill out and my head fall off - I'm not bowing down to these mental afflictions, not today or any day.

44. A regular enemy might escape to another country and come back stronger, but these mental afflictions? Once they're gone, where are they gonna go?

45. Once they're out of my mind, what's their next move? Where will they rest? How will they plan their comeback? I've been weak, but with wisdom's eye, these afflictions aren't as tough as they seem.

46. These afflictions don't exist in what we see, our senses, or anywhere in between. So where are they, causing all this drama? It's all illusion, baby. Free your scared heart and serve that wisdom. Why torture yourself for nothing?

47. After thinking it through like this, I better werk these teachings exactly as explained. If you could be cured by medicine but ignore your doctor's advice, how are you ever gonna heal?

5. Keeping Your Inner House in Check

1. If I want to protect my spiritual practice, honey, I better guard that mind like it's my most precious designer piece - because without keeping that messy mind in check, my practice is going nowhere but down.

2. A regular elephant throwing a tantrum in the zoo can't cause half the damage of the untamed elephant of my mind - we're talking depths-of-hell level destruction, sweetie.

3. But if I can keep that wild mind-elephant tied down with the rope of mindfulness[27], all my fears will sashay away and every virtue will fall right into my perfectly manicured hands.

4. Tigers, lions, elephants, bears, snakes, and every other enemy I can think of - even those hell realm security guards...

5. All those evil spirits and demons get in formation the moment I get my mind under control - tame that mind and everything else falls in line.

6. The ultimate queen of truth spilled the tea herself - every

---

[27] Mindfulness: The practice of maintaining awareness of the present moment, including one's thoughts, actions, and surroundings.

single fear and endless suffering starts right here in this messy mind of ours.

7. Who's out there crafting all those weapons in hell? Who laid down that burning iron floor? And where did all those temptresses come from?

8. The wise one said all that drama comes straight from an evil mind - so in all three realms of existence, there's nothing fiercer or more dangerous than this mind of ours.

9. If perfect generosity actually meant eliminating poverty in the world, how come we still have poor people after all those enlightened beings practiced it?

10. The real tea about perfect generosity is this: it's all about the genuine intention to give everything away to everyone, plus all the good karma that comes with that thought.

11. Where can I possibly take fish where killing won't happen? But when I genuinely decide to give up killing, that's what we call perfect ethical realness.

12. How many shady people can I actually take down? They're as endless as space itself. But slay that angry mindset, and I've won every battle there is.

13. Where are you gonna find enough leather to cover the whole earth? Just wear shoes, honey - same difference.

14. Same with trying to control everything out there in the world - it's not gonna happen. But if I can just keep this mind in check, what else needs controlling?

15. Even with all the body language and vocal fry in the world, if my mind isn't serving clarity, I'm not getting those high-realm results that a clear mind gets all by itself.

16. The all-knowing one said all my chanting and spiritual austerities are about as useful as last season's trends if my mind is somewhere else or just not feeling it.

17. Those who haven't worked on their minds - which is the real gag and essence of dharma - are just wandering around in circles trying to find happiness and dodge suffering.

18. So I better keep this mind controlled and protected like it's my most precious possession. Once I drop that commitment to guarding my mind, what's the point of any other promises?

19. Just like you'd protect a fresh wound when you're in the middle of a rowdy crowd, protect your mind when you're surrounded by messy energy.

20. If I'm so careful about protecting a tiny wound because it might hurt, why aren't I guarding my mind when it could get crushed by mountains in hell?

21. With this fierce mindset, even surrounded by shady people and temptations, a determined queen will stay undefeated through persistent effort.

22. Let everything else go - my stuff, my reputation, this body, my job, all of it can sashay away. But this virtuous mind? That's the one thing I'm keeping, honey.

23. Listen up, all you spiritual divas trying to guard your minds: keep that mindfulness and self-reflection on point like it's your signature look.

24. Just like someone too sick to werk, a mind without mindfulness and introspection isn't fit to serve anything.

25. Everything you've learned and practiced is like water in a cracked glass - it all leaks out when your mind isn't paying attention to what it's doing.

26. Even the most devoted queens with endless stamina can get messy with bad habits if they're not watching their own minds.

27. You can stack up good karma like designer shoes, but if you let that thief of unconsciousness rob you after losing your mindfulness, you're headed straight for the basement of existence.

28. These mental afflictions are like a gang of thieves casing the joint - once they find a way in, they'll snatch all the good fortune from your life faster than you can say "security!"

29. That's why mindfulness needs to stay at my mind's entrance like the fiercest bouncer at the club. If it steps away, bring it back by remembering what hell feels like.

30. Mindfulness comes naturally when you've got a fabulous spiritual mentor in your corner and you're living for their wisdom - partly from respect, partly from knowing they'll read you for filth if you stray.

31. The Buddhas and Bodhisattvas are serving omniscient realness in every direction - nothing escapes their gaze, and here I am, feeling seen.

32. When I'm meditating like this, keep it proper and respectful with just a touch of healthy fear, and keep those enlightened beings on my mind like they're my favorite playlist.

33. When mindfulness is working the door of my mind like a fierce bouncer, true self-reflection walks in and becomes a permanent resident.

34. First things first, I need to get my mind right and keep it as still as a mannequin in Saks Fifth Avenue.

35. Don't be serving wandering eyes without purpose - keep that gaze lowered like you're studying the runway.

36. But honey, do look around occasionally to rest those eyes, and if someone crosses your path, serve them a proper

greeting.

37. Check all directions for danger like you're crossing West Hollywood at midnight - take a moment, look ahead, and only check behind after you've turned around properly.

38. Whether you're moving forward or backing up, make sure you know what needs to be done before you make your next move.

39. Keep checking your posture like you're working a photo-shoot - and periodically strike a fresh pose to make sure everything's still aligned.

40. Watch that wild elephant mind of yours like it's your last designer piece, keeping it firmly tethered to that strong pillar of dharma practice[28].

41. I shall check where my mind is wandering and not let it stray from that pole of concentration even for a hot second.

42. If danger's coming for me or it's time to celebrate, I can relax those rules a bit - even ethical discipline can take five when it's time for giving.

43. Once I know what needs to be done, I'll focus on that like it's the last sale of the season - don't let anything else distract you until you've worked it out.

44. This is how I'll get everything done right. Otherwise, nothing works out and my lack of self-awareness just keeps growing like bad roots.

45. Cut out that craving for empty chatter and entertainment faster than you can say "delete account."

---

[28] Dharma practice: The active application of Buddhist teachings in one's life through study, meditation, and ethical conduct. More specific than the general term "dharma" as it refers to actual implementation.

46. If I catch myself mindlessly crushing earth, pulling up grass, or drawing in dirt, remember the Buddha's teachings and stop that behavior immediately.

47. Before I move or speak, check my mind like I'm checking my look in the mirror - then work it with grace.

48. When I clock my mind getting attached or repulsed, I'll serve absolute stillness - no moving, no speaking, just channeling that wooden energy.

49. When my mind is feeling its oats - getting sarcastic, conceited, arrogant, shady, evasive, or straight-up deceptive...

50. When it wants to brag or throw shade at others, getting all heated and irritable, that's my cue to serve wooden realness again.

51. When my mind is thirsting for coins, fame, and followers, or demanding to be waited on hand and foot, keep serving that wooden energy.

52. When my mind is giving "me, me, me" and couldn't care less about others, or when it's desperate for an audience, channel that wooden energy once more.

53. When it's getting impatient, lazy, timid, bold, chatty, or biased in my favor - you guessed it - wooden realness is the way.

54. When I catch my mind acting up or wasting time on nonsense, I'll be a hero and shut it down with whatever antidote works.

55. Work it like you mean it - confident but not cocky, steady and respectful, modest and calm, living to lift others up.

56. Don't let the messy drama of confused people get to you - serve them compassion instead, knowing their mental afflictions are making them act up.

57. I'll keep it clean for myself and others, maintaining that

humble mindset like I'm a fabulous apparition.

58. Remember how rare and precious this moment of freedom is - keep your mind as unshakeable as the fiercest mountain.

59. Why stress about vultures dragging this body around after death? If you won't object then, why make a scene now?

60. Mind, why are you so obsessed with protecting this body like it's yours? It's not even part of you - what's it doing for you anyway?

61. Oh honey, if you wouldn't claim a pristine wooden statue as your own, why are you so pressed about protecting this messy machine made of ick?

62. First, use that brilliant mind of yours to peel back this skin like you're removing last season's wallpaper, and use wisdom's knife to separate flesh from bones.

63. Crack those bones open and look at the marrow like you're judging a design challenge - where's the essence in all this?

64. If you search this thoroughly and find no essence, then spill the tea - why are you still protecting this body like it's a collectors item?

65. If you wouldn't eat this mess, drink the blood, or snack on the organs (and honey, who would?), then what's the point of this body anyway?

66. Though I suppose it's fair to keep it around to feed the vultures and jackals eventually. This human body is just a tool for getting things done, like a really complicated Swiss Army knife.

67. Even though I guard it like a bouncer at the most exclusive club, death's going to snatch this body away and serve it to the vultures anyway. What's my plan then?

68. You wouldn't waste good clothes on a temp worker who's

about to quit, right? This body's just going to eat and bounce - so why are you investing so much in it?

69. So listen up, mind - give the body its basic paycheck and focus on your own glow-up. You don't give all your coins to the help, do you?

70. Think of this body like your personal yacht - it gets you from here to there. Work it however you need to serve all beings' happiness.

71. Once you've got this kind of control, keep your face serving joy like it's a permanent Instagram filter. Drop the RBF, be the first to say hey, and be everyone's judy.

72. Don't be throwing furniture around like you're on a reality show. Don't be slamming doors either - silence is the new black.

73. Take notes from the crane, the cat, and the thief - they move quiet and sneaky to get what they want. That's how a wise queen should move.

74. Take direction from those who know how to lead and help others without being asked - be everybody's student, because learning is fundamental.

75. Show appreciation for all the good words out there. When you see someone serving virtue, hype them up like they're your favorite performer.

76. Spill the tea about others' good qualities when they're not around, and when someone's praising your virtues, take it as appreciation for excellence in general.

77. Everything we do is for satisfaction, which is harder to get than a callback from my crush. So I'm gonna get my joy from celebrating other people's fierce accomplishments.

78. This way, I'm not losing anything in this life, and I'm setting myself up for future happiness. But holding

grudges? That's just suffering now and major drama later.

79. Keep your voice soft and sweet like a lullaby - speak truth that makes sense, is clear as crystal, pleasant to hear, and comes from a place of love.

80. Look at all beings like they're the most gorgeous thing you've ever seen, thinking "thanks to these queens, I'm gonna reach enlightenment."

81. Major blessings come from constantly thirsting after opportunities for virtue and kindness, and from being the antidote to others' suffering.

82. I'll be skilled and fierce, and do the work myself - don't be passing the opportunity to someone else like it's a hot potato.

83. The perfections get more and more elevated as you go along - don't drop a higher one for a lower one unless it fits with the bodhisattva way of life.

84. Understanding this, I'll always work for others' benefit. Even the "don't go there" stuff is allowed if I've got the compassion and can see it'll help.

85. I'll share my food with those in rough situations, those without protection, and spiritual seekers. Keep my portions modest. Keep just the clothes I need and give everything else away like it's the end-of-season clearance.

86. Don't wreck this body that practices the deep dharma just for some minor benefit - this body is my ticket to fulfilling all beings' hopes real quick.

87. When my compassion isn't pure yet, I won't go sacrificing my life - I'll save that for when my mind is truly unbiased. Don't waste this precious existence, honey.

88. I won't be dropping profound dharma wisdom when someone's being shady and disrespectful. And honey,

if someone struts in like they own the place - acting all entitled with their designer accessories, status symbols, or aggressive attitude - or can't even be bothered to take off their baseball cap, that's not the time for sacred wisdom.

89. I won't spill this spiritual tea to those who aren't ready to drink it. I'll make sure my teaching space is safe and appropriate for everyone. And honey, don't be throwing shade at any level of dharma practice - it's all fierce!

90. Don't try to push someone who's ready for the full enlightenment fantasy back into spiritual basic training. And don't distract them from their bodhisattva journey by tempting them with trendy mindfulness apps and spiritual quick-fixes.

91. I won't be messy with your toothbrush or spitting, and won't use water or usable land as your personal bathroom - that's just tacky.

92. Don't eat like you're at an all-you-can-eat buffet - no talking with my mouth full, no noise, no gaping mouth. Keep those legs tucked and don't be rubbing my hands together like a villain.

93. I shall avoid putting myself in situations that read as sketchy or inappropriate. I will check what makes people uncomfortable and avoid it like last year's trends.

94. I won't point with one finger like I'm accusing someone - I'll serve directions with my whole right hand, and make it elegant.

95. I won't be hollering and waving my arms unless it's urgent - a finger snap will do just fine. Otherwise, I'm just losing my composure for nothing.

96. When I sleep, I'll work that lion pose like the enlightened ones did for nirvana. Waking up fierce and ready, with

my intentions set.

97. The bodhisattva way has more variations than a drag queen's wardrobe. I'll start with the practices that clean up my mind first.

98. Three times during the day and three times at night, I'll recite that three-part prayer. It'll help clear those slip-ups through my connection with the enlightened ones and that awakened mindset.

99. Apply yourself to whatever training fits your situation, whether you chose it or life chose it for you.

100. There's nothing the spiritual children shouldn't learn - when you're working it this way, everything becomes virtuous.

101. Everything I do should benefit beings, directly or indirectly. Make it all work for enlightenment, but make it all about helping others.

102. Never ghost your spiritual friend who is living that bodhisattva life and knows their enlightenment stuff - not even if the tea gets scalding hot!

103. Learn how to respect your teachers from the "The Revolutionary Life of Frida Kahlo" by Pema Chödrön - she spills all the authentic relationship tea.

104. The practices are all mapped out in "When Things Fall Apart" or "Start Where You Are" - Miss Pema's got you covered like the best setting powder.

105. Make Sharon Salzberg's "Lovingkindness" your bedtime reading - it's got all the details about serving proper conduct.

106. Or start with Jack Kornfield's "The Wise Heart" for the highlight reel before diving into "The Heart of the Buddha's Teaching" by Thich Nhat Hanh - that's the

platinum collection, darling.

107. See what's yasss and what's no-no, then work those teachings to protect everyone's minds.

108. Here's introspection in a nutshell: keep checking your body and mind like you're doing quality control.

109. I'll do it, because just reading about it is like following a cookbook without cooking.

6. The Enlightened Quality of Patience

1. All that good karma that I built up over thousands of lifetimes - my generosity, my worship, my whole spiritual glow-up? One moment of anger burns it all down faster than a shady tweet gone viral.
2. Nothing's messier than hatred, nothing fiercer than patience. So I better werk on that patience game from every angle I've got.
3. When I've got that hatred thorn stuck in my heart, my mind's like a messy dressing room - no peace, no joy, no rest, no stability. Just pure chaos.
4. Even the people I'm supporting with my coins and my influence will come for me if I'm serving anger realness. That's the tea.
5. My friends start avoiding me like I'm wearing last season's looks. Sure, I might attract people with my generosity, but they won't stick around. Let's be real - there's nothing that makes me happy when I'm angry.
6. Once I clock hatred as the enemy, once I see all the mess it creates, and I start shutting it down? That's when I start living my best life, here and in whatever comes next.
7. Anger's like that one toxic ex who feeds off my dissatisfac-

tion - whether it's because I didn't get what I wanted, or someone's blocking my blessings. Once it gets fired up, it's coming for me.

8. So I'm cutting off anger's food supply, because this enemy's only got one job - making my life a mess.

9. Even when life's serving me nothing but problems, I won't let it steal my joy. Once I let frustration in, nothing feels right, and all my virtues sashay away.

10. If there's something I can do about it, why get frustrated? If there's nothing I can do about it, why get frustrated? Either way, frustration's not giving me life.

11. I don't want suffering, shade, reading, or disrespect coming at me or my chosen family. But when it comes to my enemies? The library is open.

12. Happiness is harder to find than size 13 heels that actually work, but suffering? That's readily available. But here's the gag - suffering is what sets me free from this whole cycle. So I need to toughen up.

13. Some folks out there are enduring all kinds of pain for their beliefs - getting burned, cut, the whole nine. If they can do all that for their faith, why am I being so precious about my journey to liberation?

14. Everything gets easier with practice. I'll start small with my pain tolerance, and before I know it, I'll be handling the big stuff like a pro.

15. I deal with thirst, hunger, bugs, rashes - all that basic nonsense - without breaking a sweat. Why am I acting brand new about this?

16. Cold, heat, rain, wind, traveling, being sick, getting locked up, getting beat down - I won't let any of it break me. The moment I start playing fragile, that's when the real

suffering begins.

17. Some queens see blood and turn into warriors, while others faint just looking at someone else's paper cut. What's the tea?

18. It's all about that mental stamina. Either I've got it or I don't. So I'll build myself up to be untouchable by suffering - make pain my backup dancer.

19. Even when I'm going through it, if I'm wise I'll keep my mind as unbothered as a drag queen's face in the rain. The real battle is with my inner saboteurs, and pain comes with the territory.

20. The true winners in life? They see suffering and they're like "whatever." They conquer real enemies like hatred. Everyone else is just playing with corpses.

21. But here's a gag about suffering - it can actually serve me. It reads my ego for filth, makes me feel for other beings, keeps me scared straight (well, maybe not straight), and makes me live for the Buddha.

22. Listen, if I don't get mad at my IBS and my period cramps that cause me pain, why am I getting pressed about people? They're just as controlled by conditions as my hormones are.

23. Just like that hangover I didn't ask for but got anyway, anger shows up uninvited and unwanted.

24. Nobody wakes up and decides "Today I'm gonna get angry!" Anger doesn't wake up and think "Time to ruin someone's day!" It just happens.

25. All these messy behaviors and vices are like a perfectly orchestrated performance - they need all the right conditions to happen. None of them can steal the show solo.

26. When all these conditions come together to create drama,

they're not plotting like the mean girls in high school. And whatever mess they create isn't trying to be born either.

27. That deep philosophical tea about some supreme self or original substance? Child, it's not sitting there planning its debut.

28. If it hasn't shown up yet, how's it gonna be planning anything? And if it's already here being messy, how's it gonna plan to stop?

29. If this "permanent self" everyone's going on about isn't even conscious, it's about as active as the void between a fake queen's ears. And even if I throw some conditions its way, what's an unchanging thing gonna do with them?

30. What's this "self" doing during all the action anyway? If it's the same before and after, what's it contributing to the party? If I'm saying it's connected to the action somehow, which one's causing which?

31. Everything's depending on something else for its moment, and even those things they're depending on aren't living their independent fantasy. So why get mad at things that are basically just special effects in this cosmic drag show?

32. Now some shady queen might say "If there's no real self, then who's letting go of anger?" But honey, that's exactly the point - it's all just causes and conditions, and that's how suffering stops.

33. So next time I see my friend or enemy acting a mess, I'll just remember - they're serving realness based on their conditions. Keep it cute and unbothered.

34. If everybody got everything they wanted just by wishing, nobody would be suffering, because who's out here wishing for pain?

35. Look at these queens hurting themselves - whether it's

being careless with thorns, starving themselves out of anger, or chasing after unavailable trade.

36. Some folks are really taking it to the extreme - hanging themselves, jumping off cliffs, taking poison, living that destructive life.

37. When these mental afflictions get hold of me, I'll even come for myself. So what makes me think people have any control when it comes to throwing shade at others?

38. If I can't even feel compassion for someone who's so caught up in their mental mess that they're coming for themselves, why am I getting mad?

39. If it's just in some people's nature to be messy, getting mad at them is like getting mad at fire for being hot. What's the point?

40. If this whole drama is actually helping someone grow, and if all beings are fundamentally fierce and fabulous, then getting mad at them is like getting pressed about smoke in the sky - pointless.

41. If I'm ignoring the whole cause and effect situation - like the stick that hit me and what made it move - and just getting mad at the person swinging it, then I might as well be mad at anger itself, because that person's just being pushed around by their own anger anyway.

42. Let's keep it real - I've caused my share of pain to others in the past. So if someone's coming for me now, maybe I had it coming.

43. Their weapon and my body are both just causing pain here. They got their weapon, I got this body. So who am I supposed to be mad at in this story?

44. Driven by my thirsty desires, I ended up with this human body that's basically just a walking wound that can't handle

being touched. When it hurts, who am I really supposed to blame?

45. Here I am, not wanting to suffer but living for the drama that causes suffering. When I'm the one who created this mess, why am I trying to read someone else for filth?

46. Just like those hellish situations my karma created - you know, those razor-sharp leaves and those shady birds from hell - I brought this on myself. So who exactly am I supposed to be mad at?

47. The people throwing shade at me? They're just following the script I wrote with my own actions. And because of it, they're headed somewhere worse than the back room of the shadiest club. Look at me, ruining their lives.

48. Thanks to them, I'm getting better at patience and dropping my vices. Meanwhile, because of me, they're about to face some long-term consequences. Who's really being cruel here?

49. I'm the one causing them harm while they're actually helping me grow. So why is my messy mind trying to spin this narrative and get angry?

50. If I'm really about that virtuous life, I won't end up in those hellish places. But if I'm just looking out for myself, what's gonna happen to them?

51. If I clap back, it's not gonna help them, and I'll just mess up my own spiritual progress. That way, everyone who's already struggling just gets more lost.

52. The mind itself can't be hurt - it's not like I can punch a thought. But because it's so attached to this body like a drag queen to her foundation, it gets pressed when the body's suffering.

53. Shade, reading, and disrespect don't actually damage my

body. So why am I getting so triggered, mind?

54. Is their unkindness gonna come eat me up in this life or the next? Is that why I'm so pressed about it?

55. If I'm pressed because it's blocking my coin, honey let me tell you - those material gains are gonna vanish in this life anyway, but that negative karma? That's gonna stick around like a bad reputation.

56. Better to sashay away from this life today than live a long messy existence. Because even after living that long life, death's still gonna read me for filth in the end.

57. One queen wakes up after dreaming about a hundred years of pleasure, another after just a moment of joy. What's the difference?

58. Does either one get to keep that happiness after they wake up? It's the same tea when you die - whether you lived that long life or just had a short moment in the spotlight.

59. Even if I've collected more stuff than a drag queen's closet and lived that luxurious life, in the end I'm leaving as naked as the day I was born, like someone snatched my whole wardrobe.

60. What's the point of living off these material things if I'm destroying virtue and creating mess? Aren't I just trading spirituality for stuff when I get angry about material things?

61. If my life's purpose is getting destroyed, what's the point of living a life that's just creating bad karma?

62. I think I'm justified getting mad at someone who's dragging my name through the mud because they're hurting others? Then why aren't I pressed when other people get the same treatment?

63. I'm serving patience realness when people are being shady

65

to others, but the moment they come for me? Girl, where did all that patience go when they're clearly just caught up in their own mental mess?

64. Getting angry at people who disrespect sacred images and teachings is actually the wrong move - the Buddhas are unbothered by that drama.

65. Just like before, when people come for my spiritual mentors, family, or friends, I'll remember it's all just conditions playing out. Keep that anger in check.

66. Pain comes at me from all directions - sometimes from people, sometimes from things that aren't even conscious. The suffering happens in my mind, so that's where I need to werk on my patience.

67. Some people are messy because they're confused, others get angry because they're confused. So who's really innocent and who's guilty in this situation?

68. What kind of karma did I create before that's making people come for me now? Everyone's subject to their own actions - who am I to try and change that universal law?

69. Understanding this, I'm gonna focus on creating virtue so everyone can serve loving kindness to each other.

70. When I see fire spreading from house to house, I better grab that flammable stuff and get it out of there real quick.

71. Same way, when my mind's on fire with hatred because of attachment, I'll throw that mess out immediately before it burns up all my spiritual good karma.

72. If someone's about to get executed but gets away with just losing a hand, is that really unfortunate? If someone escapes hell by dealing with some human-realm drama, is that really such a bad deal?

73. If I can't even handle this basic level suffering happening

right now, why aren't I working harder to get rid of anger? That's what's gonna lead to some real suffering in hell.

74. Because of anger alone, I've been serving hell realness thousands of times, and it hasn't done anything good for me or anyone else.

75. But this current suffering hits different - it can bring great benefits. The only suffering worth living for is the kind that helps eliminate everyone else's suffering.

76. If others are living their best life praising someone's good qualities, why aren't I joining that celebration, mind?

77. This joy from celebrating others is pure happiness without the hangover. The enlightened ones are here for it, and it's the best way to bring people together.

78. If I'm not feeling it because I think it only makes them happy, then by that logic, I should stop paying people too - but then I'd lose all my good karma, seen and unseen.

79. When people are praising my good qualities, I want everyone to join the party. But when they're praising someone else? I won't even let myself feel happy about it.

80. I generated this enlightened mindset because I wanted all beings to be happy. So why am I mad now that they're actually finding some happiness on their own?

81. If I'm all about wanting beings to reach that Buddha-level fabulousness that even the gods bow down to, why am I getting so heated when they receive a little recognition?

82. When someone nurtures a person I should be nurturing, they're doing me a favor. If someone's supporting my chosen family, why am I serving jealousy instead of gratitude?

83. If I'm claiming to want enlightenment for all beings, how can I be mad at their success? That enlightened mindset

and jealousy don't go together like that.

84. If someone doesn't get that gift and it stays with the giver, I wasn't getting it anyway. So why am I pressed about whether they give it away or not? Make it make sense.

85. Why would I want anyone to block their blessings, push away kind people, or dim their own light? If someone's receiving gifts, what's really triggering me?

86. Not only am I not owning up to my own mess, but I'm trying to compete with others who are actually doing the work? The audacity!

87. If something bad happens to my enemy, does my satisfaction make it happen twice? My wishes alone aren't manifesting anything without a cause.

88. Even if my shady wishes could cause someone's suffering, why would I live for that? If I say it makes me happy, there's nothing more tragic than that kind of joy.

89. Once these mental afflictions catch me like a fish on their hook, those hell realm guards are gonna have me simmering in their infernal pressure cooker realness.

90. All that praise, fame, and status isn't doing anything for my spiritual glow-up, my longevity, my strength, my health, or my physical slay.

91. If I'm really looking out for my own interests, what good is all that? If I just want mental pleasure, I might as well go all in on gambling and drinking.

92. Some queens will throw away their coins and even their lives for fame - but what good are empty words? When you're dead, who's enjoying that reputation?

93. When I lose praise and fame, my mind acts like a toddler whose sandcastle just got knocked over - and that's not the look I'm going for.

94. Words aren't conscious beings - they can't actually praise me. I'm just getting my life because I know someone likes me.

95. Whether it's for someone else or for me, what's someone else's affection really giving me? Their joy belongs to them - I don't even get a sample size portion of it.

96. If I'm gonna celebrate someone else's joy, I should be doing it across the board. Why am I getting salty when others are living their best life because someone else is favoring them?

97. The truth is, I'm just feeling myself because I'm being praised. But let's be real - that's some kindergarten behavior.

98. Praise and recognition are just distracting me from seeing how messy this cycle of existence is. They're stirring up jealousy toward talented people and anger at their success.

99. So aren't the people trying to destroy my reputation actually keeping me from falling into hell? Now that's a plot twist!

100. These chains of material gain and honor aren't the look for someone seeking liberation. How can I hate the ones who are helping me break free?

101. How can I be mad at those who, like they're blessed by the Buddha themselves, are blocking my entrance to the suffering I'm trying to serve?

102. It's not right to get heated at someone thinking they're blocking my merit. Since there's no spiritual practice fiercer than patience, shouldn't I be working that?

103. If I'm not serving patience because of my own issues, then I'm the one creating obstacles when I could be creating merit. That's the gag.

104. If something can't exist without something else, and shows up when that thing is present, then that thing is its cause. How am I calling it an obstacle?

105. A person asking for help isn't blocking generosity when I'm giving - they're enabling it. When someone shows up to ordain me, we don't call them an obstacle to ordination.

106. People asking for help are easy to find in this world, but those who wrong us? That's rare, because no one's coming for you if you're not serving drama.

107. So since my enemies are helping me werk this bodhisattva path, I should treasure them like finding designer vintage in my closet that I forgot I had.

108. We both got the gift of patience out of this - and they should get the credit first, because they made it possible.

109. If I'm saying they don't deserve respect because they weren't trying to help me develop patience, then why do I honor the dharma? It's not trying to help us either.

110. If I'm not respecting adversaries because they're trying to harm me, then why would I have patience with them if they're actually like doctors trying to help me?

111. Patience only shows up because of that harmful intention, so they're the ones making it possible. I should respect them just like I respect the dharma - and that's the tea.

112. The wise ones said that all beings are like the Buddha's garden, because so many have reached enlightenment by serving them.

113. Since both beings and Buddhas are equally responsible for helping us get those Buddha qualities, why aren't I respecting beings the same way I respect the Buddhas?

114. Their greatness isn't about their intentions but about the results. Regular beings can create the same results, so

they're equal in that way.

115. The power to inspire friendship and respect - that's what makes beings great. The merit that comes from faith in the Buddhas - that's what makes the Buddhas great.

116. So beings and Buddhas are equal when it comes to helping us get those Buddha qualities. But nobody's on the same level as the Buddhas when it comes to their endless good qualities.

117. If I find even a tiny drop of those essential good qualities in someone, three whole worlds wouldn't be enough to honor them properly.

118. Since beings have some part of those fierce Buddha qualities, it's right to honor them just for that family resemblance.

119. Besides respecting beings, how else can I repay these true friends who help us beyond measure?

120. The kindness of bodhisattvas who give up their lives and enter hell realms is repaid by serving beings. So even if beings come for me, I'll serve them nothing but kindness.

121. Why am I getting all high and mighty instead of serving these masters who my spiritual guides would die for?

122. The wise ones live for others' joy and can't stand to see them hurt. Make them happy and all the sages are gagged with joy - hurt them and I'm coming for the sages themselves.

123. Just like I can't enjoy anything when my body's on fire, these compassionate ones can't be happy when beings are suffering.

124. So today I'm confessing all the shade I've thrown at these great compassionate ones by hurting beings. May the wise ones forgive me for not keeping them pleased.

125. To make the enlightened ones happy, I'm putting my whole self in service to the world today. Let people walk all over me, let them read me for filth - as long as it pleases the World's Protector.

126. There's no question that these Compassionate Ones see all beings as themselves. Don't we see them showing up as regular beings to protect us? So why aren't I serving them proper respect?

127. This is the only thing that makes the enlightened ones gag. This is the only way to serve my purpose. This is the only thing that snatches away the world's suffering. So this is the only thing I'm committing to.

128. When some king's enforcer is terrorizing the people, those who can see the bigger picture know they can't clap back.

129. Because that person isn't working alone - they've got the king's power behind them. So I won't come for someone who seems weak when they've done wrong.

130. Because their power comes from both the hell realm guards and the Compassionate Ones. So I'll serve beings like I'd serve a temperamental king.

131. What could an angry king do that would match the hell realm drama I'd get from causing mental pain to beings?

132. What could a happy king give me that would equal the enlightenment I'd get from making beings happy?

133. Never mind future Buddha realness - can't I see how serving beings leads to fortune, fame, and happiness right here and now?

134. A patient person moving through lives serves beauty, health, and charisma.

7. The Enlightened Quality of Joyous Effort

1. Once we've got that patience down, honey, it's time to serve some spiritual enthusiasm. Without joyous effort, or zeal, we're not getting to enlightenment - just like nothing moves without wind, we're not creating merit without some spiritual motivation.
2. What's zeal? It's living for virtue like it's the last sale at Barneys. What kills it? Spiritual laziness, clinging to mess, not caring, and that "I can't" attitude.
3. That spiritual sloth comes from being lazy, chasing pleasures, sleeping too much, and wanting to lounge around because I'm not gagged by how messy this cycle of existence is.
4. These mental afflictions are hunting me down like paparazzi, and I've walked right into the trap of rebirth. How am I not seeing that I'm already in death's mouth?
5. I'm not even clocking that my own kind are being picked off one by one. I'm sleeping through it all like a buffalo surrounded by butchers.
6. With death watching me like a shady queen and every exit blocked, how am I still eating, sleeping, and hooking up

like everything's fine?

7. Death's coming faster than last season's trends, so until then, I need to stack up that merit and wisdom like it's going out of style. Even if I finally get it together when death shows up, it's too late to serve that energy then.

8. "I haven't done this yet... I just started that... This isn't even finished... And now death shows up? The drama of it all!"

9. Looking at my crying family with their puffy, red eyes, tears running down their faces from all that grief, and death's messengers giving me that look...

10. Tortured by remembering all my messy choices, hearing hell's soundtrack, and losing control of my body from fear - what's my plan then?

11. When I realize I'm like a fish out of water, that fear is right on schedule. But imagine how much worse it'll be when I've got some real sins to answer for and hell's heat to deal with.

12. I'm so delicate that hot water burns me - so how do I think I'm going to handle hell's temperature when I'm serving those kinds of choices?

13. I want results without effort? I'm too precious for pain but acting immortal while death's got me in its grip? Girl, I'm destroying myself!

14. Now that I've scored this rare human life realness, I'll use it to cross that river of suffering. This isn't naptime, honey, because this opportunity is harder to catch than a celebrity without makeup.

15. I'm giving up the endless joy of dharma to live for jokes and games that just cause more suffering? Make it make sense!

16. Not being apathetic, working those skills like wisdom and self-control, seeing myself and others as equal, and putting others first...

17. I'll work it without that "How could little old me ever reach enlightenment?" energy. The truth-telling Buddha spilled this tea himself:

18. "Even flies, mosquitos, bees, and worms can reach that hard-to-get enlightenment if they werk it hard enough."

19. I'm human, I know what's good for me and what isn't - so why couldn't I reach enlightenment if I'm following the all-knowing one's guidance?

20. If I'm scared thinking "Not my arms and legs!" then I'm confused about what matters because I can't tell the difference between a rhinestone and a diamond.

21. For millions of eons, I'll be cut, stabbed, burned, and split open again and again, but that won't get me enlightened.

22. But this little bit of suffering that leads to full enlightenment? It's like getting a splinter removed - a moment of ouch for a lifetime of relief.

23. All doctors have to use treatments that aren't pleasant. So to cure a whole lot of suffering, I've got to handle a little bit.

24. But this ultimate physician is different - they cure even chronic conditions with gentle methods.

25. At first, the guide has me giving away vegetables and stuff like that. I build up gradually until I can give away my own flesh without thinking twice.

26. Once I realize my flesh is no different from a vegetable, giving away my flesh and bones becomes no big deal.

27. Drop those vices and I won't suffer; get wise and my mind stays unbothered. Mental pain comes from wrong

thinking, and physical pain comes from messy actions.

28. Merit keeps my body fierce, wisdom keeps my mind joyful. What could possibly bother a compassionate queen who stays in this mess to help others?

29. When I burn away old sins and stack up oceans of merit through the power of that enlightened mindset alone, I'm passing those individual practitioners like they're standing still.

30. Once I'm riding that enlightened mindset chariot that snatches away all depression and exhaustion, what smart person would get discouraged? I'm just moving from one joy to the next!

31. The powers of aspiration, steadiness, joy, and letting go are all about helping other beings. When I'm scared of suffering, I'll generate that aspiration by thinking about all its benefits.

32. After I've snatched out everything opposing it, I'll work on increasing my enthusiasm with aspiration, confidence, joy, letting go, dedication, and determination.

33. I've got to eliminate countless faults for myself and everyone else. Even though getting rid of just one fault might take thousands of eons...

34. I need to clear out my own endless faults and everyone else's too. While it might take oceans of time to eliminate each fault, if I can't even see the beginning of progress, why isn't my heart exploding from all this suffering?

35. I need need to stack up endless good qualities for myself and others - otherwise, developing even one good quality might not happen for thousands of eons.

36. I haven't even practiced a tiny fraction of good qualities. The gag is, I somehow got this precious life and wasted it.

37. I haven't found joy in celebrating and making offerings to the blessed one. I haven't respected the teachings or helped the poor.

38. I haven't helped scared people feel safe or comforted those in distress. I was just a pain in my mother's womb - literally.

39. Because I didn't aspire to dharma before, I'm in this mess now. Who in their right mind would give up aspiring to dharma?

40. The wise one said aspiration is where all virtues come from, and that comes from constantly thinking about how karma ripens.

41. Misery, depression, all kinds of fears, and blocked desires - that's what I get when I serve negativity.

42. But when I'm intentionally virtuous, wherever I go, I'll be celebrated with all the perks of my good karma.

43. But when messy people try to chase happiness, their own negative actions snatch it away with weapons of suffering.

44. Thanks to their virtues, the Buddha's children get born in these gorgeous, fragrant, cool lotus flowers, serving radiance enhanced by the Buddha's sweet voice, their beautiful bodies emerging from lotuses bloomed by the sage's light.

45. But because of negative actions, I end up screaming in pain, getting my skin snatched off by death's agents, getting dunked in molten copper, having my flesh carved off by hundreds of burning weapons, and falling on super-heated iron ground again and again.

46. So I'll nurture that aspiration for virtue like it's my signature look, working it with respect. Once I start, I'll build that confidence using the method from the

QUEERING SHANTIDEVA'S THE WAY OF THE BODHISATTVA

Vajradhvaja Sutra.
47. I'll check my resources before I start anything. Better not to start than to start and ghost halfway through.
48. This pattern follows me into my next life, and that kind of sin just makes suffering worse. I miss another chance to act, and nothing gets done.
49. I'll apply that confidence to three things: actions, minor mental drama, and ability. "I'm the only one who can do this" - that's action confidence right there.
50. This world is too caught up in mental mess to handle its own business. So I've got to do it for them - I'm not as messy as all that.
51. Why should someone else do the grunt work while I stand there looking pretty? If I won't do it because of pride, then that pride needs to go.
52. Even a crow can act like an eagle when it's coming for a dead snake. If my mind is weak, even tiny problems feel like the end of the world.
53. When I'm feeling defeated, problems come at me easy, but when I'm lifted up and enthusiastic, even the biggest drama can't touch me.
54. So I'm keeping my mind unshakeable and turning these problems into opportunities. As long as I'm letting problems beat me, trying to conquer the three worlds is just delusion.
55. I should be overcoming everything, not letting anything overcome me. This is the confidence I need - I'm a child of the victorious lions, after all.
56. People overcome by pride are a mess and don't have real confidence - they're under pride's control. Someone truly confident doesn't let the enemy run their life.

78

57. Pride leads to miserable rebirths, and even human lives are joyless. They're serving others' leftovers, looking rough, and feeling weak.

58. Everyone looks down on them, but they're still puffed up with pride and miserable. If you call these people confident, that's just sad. What kind of confidence is that?

59. The real confident ones are victorious heroes who use their confidence to slay the enemy of pride. After they kill that growing enemy of pride, they show the world what real victory looks like.

60. Living in the middle of all this mental drama, I need to be fierce in a thousand ways and unconquerable by mental afflictions, like a lion unbothered by deer.

61. Even in major drama, my eyes don't taste flavors. Same way, when trouble comes, I won't let mental afflictions take me down.

62. Whatever I'm doing, I'll werk it with my whole heart. Get intoxicated by the action itself, like someone who can't get enough of playing their favorite game.

63. We do things to find happiness, but happiness might or might not show up. But if I'm living for the action itself, how can I be happy doing nothing?

64. In this cycle of existence, sensual pleasures never satisfy - they're like honey on a razor's edge. So how could I ever get enough of the sweet nectar of merit that ripens into pure benefit?

65. So even when I finish something, I'll dive right back in, like an elephant scorched by the midday sun heading straight for the lake.

66. When my strength starts fading, I'll take a break so I can come back fresh later. When I've done something well, I'll

leave it wanting more.

67. I'll block those mental afflictions' attacks and come for them hard, like I'm in a sword fight with someone who knows what they're doing.

68. Just like I'd snatch up a dropped sword real quick out of fear, I'll pick up that dropped mindfulness fast while keeping those hell realms in mind.

69. Just like poison spreads through your whole body once it hits your blood, faults spread through my whole mind once they find a weak spot!

70. I'll be like someone carrying a jar of oil while swordsmen watch their every move - careful not to trip because they know death is watching.

71. So just like I'd jump up quick if a snake slithered into my lap, that's how fast I should shut down sleepiness and laziness!

72. Every time I mess up, I'll burn with regret and think: "How do I make sure this never happens again?"

73. I'll look for friends or tasks with this in mind: "How can I practice mindfulness in this situation?"

74. I'll remember those teachings about being conscientious - keep myself ready before any task comes my way.

75. Like cotton floating wherever the wind takes it, I'll surrender to my enthusiasm, and watch my spiritual powers flourish.

8. The Enlightened Quality of Mindfulness

1. Now that you've got that spiritual enthusiasm on lock, it's time to get your mind stable in meditation, honey. Because when your mind is all over the place, you're living between the teeth of those mental afflictions like it's shark week.
2. When you get your body and mind away from the drama, those distractions can't touch you. So leave that worldly mess behind, and drop those scattered thoughts like last season's trends.
3. You're not leaving the world behind because you're still thirsting after gains and status. So the wise ones say drop all that and contemplate this instead.
4. Get this tea: when you combine that peaceful mind with some fierce insight, you can snatch those mental afflictions right out. So first, get that inner peace through detachment from worldly drama and finding joy in the simple things.
5. You're not going to see these people you're attached to for thousands of lifetimes anyway - so why are you clinging to things that don't last longer than a TikTok trend?
6. When you can't see them, you're not happy and can't focus

on meditation. And even when you do see them, you're still not satisfied - you're just tormented by wanting more, like always.

7. You're not seeing reality and you've lost that healthy disgust with samsara's mess. You're consumed by grief - always thirsting for your faves to keep you company.

8. Thinking about them makes your precious life slip away faster than a Twitter cancellation. You're trading eternal dharma for something more temporary than a Snapchat story.

9. If you're acting just like these messy people, you're definitely headed for some lower realm drama. They can't stand someone different - so what's the point of hanging with fools?

10. One minute they're your best judy, next minute they're your sworn enemy. When they should be happy, they get mad instead. Regular folks are harder to please than a demanding drag mother.

11. Give them good advice and they get heated. They try to keep you from doing what's right. Don't listen to their mess? They get mad and set themselves up for some hell realm realness.

12. They're jealous of anyone above them, competing with their equals, looking down on those below, getting cocky from praise, and heated from criticism. Tell me again what good comes from hanging with fools?

13. Put two fools together and something messy is bound to happen - they'll be bragging about themselves, reading

others for filth, and living for all that samsaric[29] drama.

14. So hanging with others just brings problems. I'm gonna live my best life alone with a mind that's not caught up in afflictions.

15. Run far from fools like they're carrying last year's bag. Be nice to people you meet, but keep it professional - serve that kind, impartial energy without getting too close.

16. Like a bee taking nothing but nectar from flowers, I'm just here for what helps my dharma practice. I'll move through life without getting attached, like I just materialized out of nowhere.

17. When someone's thinking "I'm rich, I'm respected, everyone lives for me," that's when the fear of death is coming for them hardest.

18. Wherever your mind gets its jollies from pleasures, that's where a thousand sufferings are waiting to pop out like a surprise performance.

19. That's why the wise ones aren't living for that. Fear comes from wanting things, but it passes on its own. Get strong and look at it like you're unbothered.

20. Plenty of people have gotten rich and famous, but where are they now? Nobody knows where they went with all their coins and clout.

21. If others are reading me for filth, why should I gag when I'm praised? If they're living for me, why should I get pressed when I'm criticized?

22. If even the enlightened ones couldn't please all these beings

---

[29] Samsaric: Relating to samsara, the endless cycle of birth, death, and rebirth driven by karma and mental afflictions. The state of existence marked by suffering and dissatisfaction.

with their different attitudes, how could little old messy me? So why am I trying to make the world happy?

23. They come for you when you're poor and drag you when you're rich. How are you supposed to find joy with people who bring nothing but suffering?

24. The enlightened ones spilled this tea: a fool isn't anyone's friend, because a fool's affection never comes without an agenda.

25. Love that comes from self-interest is just loving yourself - like how losing your stuff only hurts because you're losing the pleasure it brings.

26. Trees don't read you and you can't make them happy no matter how hard you try. When will I get to live with that kind of drama-free company?

27. When will I get to live in a cave, an empty temple, or under a tree, not looking back and not attached to anything?

28. When will I get to live freely without attachment in those wide-open spaces that nobody's claimed?

29. When will I live with just my basic bowl and thrift store realness that nobody else wants, feeling fierce even with nothing to hide behind?

30. When will I visit the charnel grounds[30] and compare this decaying body of mine with the other corpses?

31. Because this body's going to get so rank that even the jackals won't come near it because of the stench.

32. If the flesh and bones that came with this body are going to fall apart and scatter, what makes you think other

---

[30] Charnel grounds: Traditional cremation and burial grounds in ancient India where practitioners would meditate on impermanence and death. Important location for contemplative practice in Buddhist tradition.

relationships will last any longer?

33. You come into this world alone and you leave it alone. Nobody else can share your suffering. So what's the point of loved ones who just get in the way?

34. Just like someone on a journey crashes at a hotel, that's how beings traveling through samsara crash in different rebirths.

35. Until four people are carrying you out while everyone's crying, you should retire to the forest like it's your personal retreat.

36. When you live alone without getting too close or too messy with anyone, and people already count you as gone, nobody's going to cry when you actually leave.

37. There's no one around to bring the drama or hurt you, and no one to distract you from remembering the Buddha and all that good stuff.

38. So I'm always going to live alone in this gorgeous forest that keeps it simple, keeps it light, and keeps all that distraction away.

39. Free from all other concerns and focused like a laser beam, I'm going to werk that meditation and get this mind under control.

40. Dropping everything else and keeping my mind focused on one thing, I'm going to balance and tame this mind. In this life and the next, these sensual desires are nothing but trouble - we're talking murder, jail time, and dismemberment now, and hell realms later.

41. That person you sent all those messages to, the one you'd do anything for, not caring about sin or shame...

42. The one you risked it all for and wrecked your health over, holding them close with so much pleasure...

43. They're just bones, honey - nothing personal about it. Why aren't you running toward liberation and holding onto that with your whole heart?

44. Either you've seen that shy, lowered face before when they finally looked up, or you haven't seen it because it was covered.

45. That face that's got you so bothered now - you'll see it uncovered when the vultures get to it. So why are you running away now?

46. You were so protective of their face, not letting anyone else look at it. So why aren't you protecting it now while it's being eaten?

47. When you see this flesh being eaten by vultures and other creatures, are you still going to decorate someone else's food with flowers, sandalwood, and jewelry?

48. You're scared of a skeleton that doesn't move when you see it like this. So why are you scared when it does move, like it's some kind of ghost?

49. Their spit and their waste come from the same food. So why are you grossed out by the waste but living for sucking face?

50. Not feeling those soft cotton pillows, but these thirsty ones, confused about what's actually gross, are saying the body doesn't stink?

51. These thirsty, messy, confused ones are throwing shade at soft cotton because "you can't have sex with it."

52. You say you're not lusting after filth, but why are you wrapping your arms around another skeleton that's just tied together with tendons and plastered with meat?

53. You've got plenty of your own mess to deal with, but here you are, craving the filth in someone else's flesh sack.

54. Ignoring a fresh lotus blooming under clear skies, your filth-obsessed mind is living for a container of muck? Make it make sense.

55. The mind you're thirsting after can't be seen or touched, and the body you can touch isn't conscious. So why are you embracing nothing but delusion?

56. It's not shocking that you can't see other people's bodies as the mess they are, but how are you not clocking your own body's nastiness?

57. You're thinking "I'm living for this flesh" and want to touch and see it. So why aren't you feeling the same way about a corpse? It's just as unconscious.

58. If you won't touch dirt because it's got waste on it, why are you trying to touch the body that produced that waste in the first place?

59. If you're not passionate about what's impure, why are you embracing someone else who came from filth, grew in filth, and was fed by filth?

60. You're not feeling a dirty worm that comes from filth because it's tiny, but you're living for a body that's full of even more filth and born from it too?

61. Not only are you unbothered by your own mess, but you're actually craving other sacks of waste.

62. Even the ground is considered nasty when you spit out or throw up delicious food like camphor or seasoned rice.

63. If you still can't trust that this is filth when it's right in your face, go look at those other bodies thrown out in the charnel grounds.

64. If you know major fear comes when the skin gets torn off, how can you still be attracted to that same thing?

65. That fragrance you're smelling is from sandalwood, not

the body. So why are you attracted to someone because of a scent that belongs to something else?

66. If you're not attracted to natural funk, isn't that good? Why are people living for worthless things just because they're covered in perfume?

67. If it's sandalwood that smells sweet, did that come from the body? Why are you attracted to someone because of a scent that belongs to something else?

68. If a naked body full of filth, with its overgrown hair and nails and yellow teeth, is scary in its natural state...

69. Why are you polishing it up like a weapon for self-destruction? This world is full of delusional people working overtime to fool themselves!

70. If you're repulsed seeing skeletons in the charnel ground, why are you attracted to a village that's just a charnel ground full of walking skeletons?

71. That filth doesn't come free - you've got to work yourself to exhaustion and suffer in hell to get it.

72. A child can't stack coins, so what's there to be happy about when you're young? If you spend your life chasing wealth, what good is pleasure when you're old?

73. Some basic sensualists work themselves to death all day, then come home so exhausted they fall asleep like corpses.

74. Others are suffering from constant travel, missing their partners and kids for years at a time.

75. Confused by desires, they sell themselves for things they never get. Instead, their lives are wasted working for other people.

76. The partners of these people who've sold themselves end up giving birth under trees in the jungle and other messy places.

77. To make a living they go to war risking their lives, or become servants to keep their pride. They're fools getting dragged for their desires.

78. Some other pleasure-seekers get mutilated, impaled on stakes, burned alive, and stabbed to death.

79. Look at wealth as endless trouble because of all the drama of getting it, keeping it, and losing it. When you're distracted by wanting wealth, you can't break free from samsara's suffering.

80. So these pleasure-seekers have tons of stress and barely any joy, like an animal with one bite of grass while pulling a heavy wagon.

81. For that tiny bit of pleasure that even animals can get, these unfortunate ones have wasted this precious human life that's harder to find than a vintage designer at a thrift store.

82. Sensual pleasure definitely doesn't last and throws you into hell realms - and for what? You're constantly exhausted for no good reason.

83. With even a billionth of that effort, you could reach enlightenment. These pleasure-seekers suffer more than spiritual practitioners but don't get any closer to awakening.

84. When you think about hell realm suffering, weapons, poison, fire, cliffs, and enemies don't even compare to sensual desires.

85. Getting over those sensual desires like that, find your joy in the peaceful forest where there's no drama or annoyances.

86. The fortunate ones thinking about how to help others wander around, touched by gentle forest breezes, cooled by moonlight reflecting off giant rocks like they're made of sandalwood.

87. In an empty hut, under a tree, or in a cave, stay as long as you want. Drop the stress of protecting your stuff and live that carefree life.

88. Living free, unattached, and unbothered by anyone, you get to taste that contentment that even kings can't find.

89. After thinking about all these benefits of solitude, calm those scattered thoughts and cultivate that enlightened mindset.

90. First, get serious about meditating on how you and others are equal: "Everyone experiences suffering and happiness the same way, so I need to protect them like I protect myself."

91. Even though it's got different parts like arms and legs, we protect the whole body. Same way, different beings with their joys and sorrows are all equal in wanting happiness, just like me.

92. Even though my pain doesn't hurt anyone else's body, I can't handle that suffering because I'm clinging to it as "mine."

93. Same way, even though others' suffering doesn't happen to me, their suffering is hard for them because they're clinging to it as "theirs."

94. I should snatch away others' suffering because it's suffering, just like my own. I should take care of others because I'm a sentient being too.

95. When happiness matters just as much to others as it does to me, what makes me so special that I only chase happiness for myself?

96. When fear and suffering are just as nasty for others as they are for me, what makes me so special that I only protect myself?

97. If I'm not protecting them because their suffering doesn't affect me, why do I protect this body from future suffering that isn't happening to me now?

98. Thinking I'll experience that future suffering is wrong - the one who dies is born somewhere else as someone else.

99. If you think everyone should handle their own suffering because foot pain isn't hand pain, why should one take care of the other?

100. If you're saying that even though it doesn't make sense, it happens because we grasp at a self, then our response is: avoid what doesn't make sense with all your might, whether it's about yourself or others.

101. The stream of consciousness, like a series of moments, and these collections of parts, like an army - none of it's real. Since there's no actual "someone" experiencing suffering, who does that suffering belong to?

102. All these sufferings are ownerless because they're all the same - they should be eliminated just because they're suffering. Why are we being picky about which ones?

103. Why prevent suffering? Because everyone agrees it's not the tea. If we're preventing it, let's prevent all of it - and if not, then that goes for everyone, not just you.

104. You might say: "But compassion causes so much suffering, why create more?" Honey, after seeing what the world goes through, how can you think compassion's suffering is too much?

105. If one person's suffering can eliminate many people's suffering, then a compassionate queen should take that on for herself and others.

106. That's why Supuspacandra[31], even knowing the king was coming for him, didn't avoid his own suffering because it would help many messy situations.

107. So someone who's trained their mind in meditation and lives to eliminate others' suffering enters hell realms like they're walking into a luxury spa.

108. When beings get liberated, there's endless joy. Isn't that enough? Why are you so pressed about your own liberation?

109. So when you're working for others' benefit, there's no ego and no despair. When you're thirsting for nothing but helping others, you're not even worried about your own karma results.

110. So just like I protect myself from shade, I'll create that same protective energy and compassion for others!

111. Because we're used to it, we think there's an "I" in these drops of blood and sperm that belong to others, even though that being doesn't actually exist.

112. So why can't I consider someone else's body as my own the same way? It's not hard to see how my own body is actually "other."

113. See yourself as full of faults and others as oceans of good qualities - then think about dropping your own identity and taking on others'.

114. Just like we cherish our hands because they're part of our body, why aren't we cherishing all beings the same way, since they're part of this world?

---

[31] Supuspacandra: A legendary bodhisattva known for sacrificing his life to teach the Dharma, exemplifying the perfection of giving. His story is often cited as an example of ultimate generosity.

115. Just like we get this idea of self about our body (which isn't actually personal) because we're used to it, couldn't we develop that same sense of identity with others?

116. When you're working for others like this, there's no ego or disappointment. Even when you feed yourself, you're not expecting a reward.

117. So just like you protect yourself from even tiny bits of shade, cultivate that same protective and compassionate energy for the whole world.

118. That's why the fierce Avalokita blessed their own name out of compassion - to snatch away even the anxiety of being in a crowd.

119. Don't run from difficulties - because of the power of habit, you might end up not even enjoying the absence of something you used to be scared to hear mentioned.

120. If you want to protect yourself and others quick, practice this secret technique of exchanging yourself for others.

121. If you get scared at even tiny dangers because you're so attached to yourself, why aren't you seeing that self as your scariest enemy?

122. Someone who kills birds, fish, and deer, setting traps because they want to cure illness or satisfy thirst and hunger...

123. Someone who kills their parents and steals from the Three Jewels for profit and respect - they're going to be fuel for the hottest hell.

124. What wise person would want, protect, or celebrate that kind of self? Who wouldn't see it as an enemy, and who would respect it?

125. If you're thinking about yourself like "If I give this away, what will I enjoy?" - that's demon energy. If you're

93

thinking about others like "If I enjoy this, what will I give away?" - that's divine realness.

126. Hurt others for your own sake? You're getting burned in hell. But give yourself some trouble for others' sake? Everything works out perfectly.

127. Wanting to build yourself up leads to messy rebirths, low status, and confusion. Transfer that same desire to someone else, and you get fortunate rebirths, respect, and wisdom.

128. Boss others around for your own benefit, and you'll end up someone's servant. But boss yourself around for others' benefit, and you'll end up in charge.

129. Everyone who's unhappy in this world got that way from wanting their own happiness. Everyone who's happy got that way from wanting others' happiness.

130. Let's cut to the chase - look at the difference between the fool who's all about themselves and the wise one who works for others.

131. If you're not trading your happiness for others' suffering, you're definitely not reaching enlightenment. How could you even find happiness in regular existence?

132. Never mind your next life - even in this one, if a servant doesn't work and a boss doesn't pay, nothing gets done.

133. When you give up creating mutual happiness and the joy of now and later, confused people create major suffering by hurting each other.

134. If all the harm, fear, and suffering in this world comes from grasping at self, what good is that great demon to me?

135. You can't avoid suffering without giving up your self, just like you can't avoid getting burned without avoiding fire.

136. So to snatch away my own suffering and others' suffering, I'm giving myself up to others and accepting others as myself.

137. Listen up, mind - make this commitment: "I belong to others." From now on, you better not care about anything but all beings' welfare.

138. It's not right to use these eyes and other senses for yourself when they're dedicated to others. It's not right to pour benefits on yourself with hands that belong to others.

139. So become a servant to all beings, and whatever you see on this body, snatch it away and use it for others' benefit.

140. Put your identity in those below you and put others' identity in yourself - cultivate envy and pride with a mind free of messy thoughts.

141. "He gets respect, not me. I'm not rich like him. He gets praised while I get read. I'm unhappy while he's living his best life."

142. "I'm doing all the work while he's relaxing. Looks like he's everything in this world while I'm nothing, no good qualities at all."

143. "What can you do without good qualities? Everyone's got some good qualities. There are some people I'm worse than, and some I'm better than."

144. "My messy ethics and views are because of these mental afflictions, not because I chose this. You need to heal me however you can, and I'll accept the pain."

145. If he can't heal me, why's he throwing shade? What good are his qualities to me when he's the one who has them?

146. He's got no compassion for beings caught in the jaws of lower realms. Plus, he's so proud of his qualities that he wants to outshine the wise ones.

147. He pretends to be equal to others just to make himself look better, and he'll use drama to get wealth and respect.

148. If everyone could see my good qualities, no one would even hear about his.

149. If my faults weren't hidden, I'd get the honor instead of him. Today I've got the goods and the glory while he's got nothing.

150. We'll watch with joy as he finally gets dragged, read for filth, and reviled from every direction.

151. And this messy one thinks he can compete with me? Does he really have my level of education, wisdom, beauty, ancestry, and wealth?

152. Hearing my qualities praised everywhere like this, I'm gagged, hair standing on end, living for this happiness.

153. Even though he's got stuff, I'll take it with my power. If he works for me, I'll give him just enough to survive.

154. We should snatch away his happiness and keep him yoked to our suffering. He's caused us drama in samsara hundreds of times.

155. Listen up, mind - you've spent countless eons trying to serve yourself, and all that work only brought you suffering.

156. So absolutely werk it this way right now, no hesitation. Later you'll see why this slays - the wise one's words are nothing but truth.

157. If you'd done this work earlier, you wouldn't be in this state without Buddha's perfection and bliss.

158. So just like you created this sense of "me" from other people's blood and sperm, think about others the same way.

159. Live like you belong to others and snatch away whatever

you see on this body - practice what helps others.

160. Get envious of yourself like this: "I'm doing fine while they're struggling; they're low while I'm high; they're working while I'm not."

161. Take away your own happiness and expose yourself to others' suffering. Check your own mess like "What did I do and when did I do it?"

162. Take someone else's mistake on yourself, and spill even your tiniest mistakes to the Great Sage.

163. Let your reputation get outshined by hyping up others, and like the humblest servant, commit yourself to everyone's benefit.

164. This messy one shouldn't be praised for temporary good qualities. Make sure no one knows about their good qualities.

165. Bottom line: whatever shade you threw at others for your own benefit, let it come back on you for the benefit of beings.

166. Don't encourage this one to be nasty - they should serve shy bride realness, modest, gentle, and controlled.

167. Act like this! Stay like this! Don't do that! You need to be checked and controlled if you step out of line.

168. Mind, if you're not doing this even when I'm telling you, then I'm coming for you alone because all the mess starts with you.

169. Where do you think you're going? I see you, and I'm about to destroy all your vanity. That was then, when you were ruining me.

170. Now drop this "But what about my interests?" fantasy. Since you don't care about all this suffering, I've sold you to others.

171. If I don't joyfully offer you to beings, you're definitely going to hand me over to the hell realm guards.

172. You've been serving me up like that and tormenting me for ages. Remembering those grudges, I'm destroying you, you self-serving mess.

173. If you're feeling yourself, you shouldn't be pleased with yourself. If you need protection, you shouldn't be protecting yourself.

174. The more you pamper this body, the more delicate and messy it gets.

175. When it's that messed up, even this whole earth can't satisfy its wants. So who's going to satisfy it?

176. Want the impossible and you get mental afflictions and disappointment. Drop the expectations and everything prospers.

177. So don't let these bodily desires run wild. It's better not to take what you want.

178. This awful, messy form ends up as ashes and stillness, moved by others. Why am I claiming it as mine?

179. What good is this contraption to me, dead or alive? How is it different from a pile of dirt? Girl, you're not dropping that "I" grasping.

180. Favoring the body just stacks up useless suffering. Why love or hate something that might as well be a piece of wood?

181. Whether I take care of it or vultures eat it, it doesn't feel love or hate, so why am I so attached?

182. If this unconscious body doesn't get mad at shade or satisfied by praise, who am I working so hard for?

183. People who like this body are called my friends. They all like their own bodies too, so why don't I like them?

184. So I've given up this body with no attachment for the world's benefit. Even though it's got lots of faults, I keep it as a tool for that work.

185. So enough of this worldly mess! Remembering the consciousness teachings and fighting off sleepiness and laziness, I'm following the wise ones.

186. So pulling my mind away from messy paths, I'll always focus it on its meditation object to clear away those obscurations.

9. The Enlightened Quality of Wisdom

1. The enlightened one served this entire system for one reason only: wisdom. So if you're trying to snatch suffering away, you better develop that wisdom like it's your signature look.
2. Reality comes in two flavors - conventional and ultimate. That ultimate reality? It's beyond your mind's pay grade. What your intellect can grasp? That's just conventional realness.
3. So we've got two types of people strutting down this spiritual runway: the contemplatives and the basic folks. And honey, those contemplatives are reading the ordinary folks for filth.
4. Even among the contemplatives, the higher ones are dragging the lower ones using examples they both accept. No matter what they're trying to prove, there's always another level of fierce.
5. Regular folks are looking at things like they're permanent and real - not getting that illusion fantasy. That's where the contemplatives and the basics are throwing shade at each other.
6. Even the things you think you're seeing directly - forms

and such? They're established by consensus, not by facts. That consensus is as fake as thinking pure things are impure.

7. The Buddha taught concepts to help people understand. And if you're coming for me saying "If these teachings are just temporary tools and not absolute truth, that's not consistent,"

8. My response is basically: No, that's not a problem at all. Spiritual practitioners understand the difference between useful conventional teachings and ultimate reality - unlike regular people who take everything at face value. If we didn't make this distinction, we'd have to accept every popular prejudice as truth (like the sexist idea that women are impure).

9. "But how can there be merit from an illusory Buddha? And if beings are like illusions, why do they keep coming back after death?" Child, let me tell you something...

10. Even an illusion lasts as long as its conditions are serving. Why should a being be truly real just because their story goes on for a while?

11. "But if consciousness isn't real, there's no sin in killing an illusion-person." Wrong, sweetie - when you've got that illusion of consciousness, virtue and vice are very much giving what they're supposed to give.

12. "An illusory mind isn't possible because mantras can't produce it." Please - different conditions create different illusions. No single thing can produce everything.

13. "If you can be ultimately free but conventionally keep transmigrating, even the Buddha would be transmigrating. So what's the point of this bodhisattva path?"

14. When conditions aren't destroyed, the illusion keeps

serving. When conditions stop, it doesn't even show up conventionally.

15. "But if even wrong perception doesn't exist, what's recognizing the illusion?"

16. If you're saying the illusion itself doesn't exist, what are you perceiving? Even if it's just an aspect of mind, in reality it's something else entirely.

17. "If mind itself is an illusion, what's perceiving what?" The world's protector already spilled this tea - mind doesn't perceive mind. Like a sword can't cut itself, mind can't clock itself.

18. "But it illuminates itself, like a lamp!" Wrong again - a lamp doesn't illuminate itself because darkness never covered it in the first place.

19. "A blue thing doesn't need something else to be blue, like a crystal does. So some things need others to happen, some don't."

20. Just like non-blueness, blue isn't its own cause. What kind of blue could make itself blue? Make it make sense.

21. "They say a lamp illuminates once awareness knows it. So what's knowing the mind when it illuminates?"

22. If nobody's perceiving whether mind is luminous or not, this conversation is as useful as discussing a barren woman's daughter's beauty.

23. "If there's no self-awareness, how do you remember consciousness?" Memory comes from connecting to something else you experienced, like rat poison's effects.

24. "It illuminates itself because mind with other conditions perceives." A jar seen through magic ointment isn't the ointment itself, darling.

25. We're not coming for how things are seen, heard, or

known. We're dragging the concept that they truly appear as they seem - that's what's causing all the suffering.

26. If you think an illusion isn't different or non-different from mind, then if it's real, how is it not different? And if it's not different, how is it real?

27. Just like you can see an illusion even though it's not real, same goes for the observer - the mind. "But samsara must have some real basis, otherwise it'd be like empty space."

28. How can something unreal have any power just by being based on something real? You're treating mind like it's some independent queen.

29. If mind was free from objects it perceives, every being would already be enlightened. So what's the point of claiming only mind exists?

30. "Even when you know it's like an illusion, how do mental afflictions stop? After all, the magician who creates an illusory woman can still feel lust for her."

31. Because the creator's imprints of afflictions toward objects haven't been snatched away. When he sees her, his understanding of emptiness is still giving baby queen energy.

32. Stack up those emptiness imprints and watch those existence imprints fade. Keep serving "nothing exists truly" realness until even that vanishes.

33. "If something unreal can't be perceived, how can a non-entity with no basis appear to the mind?"

34. When neither entity nor non-entity is giving face to the mind, since there's no other option, it becomes peaceful without objects.

35. Like a wish-fulfilling gem or tree satisfies desires, the Buddha's image serves because of his vow and his disciples'

connection.

36. When a poison-charmer dies after blessing a pillar, that pillar keeps neutralizing poison long after they're gone.

37. Same way, the Buddha's pillar, built according to the bodhisattva blueprint, keeps working even after the bodhisattva has sashayed into nirvana.

38. "How can offerings to something unconscious bear fruit?" Because it's taught that it works the same whether Buddha's serving presence or nirvana.

39. Scripture says worship brings results, conventionally or ultimately, just like offerings to the actual Buddha are fruitful.

40. "Liberation comes from understanding the four noble truths[32], so why bother with emptiness?" Because scripture says there's no awakening without this path, honey.

41. "The Mahayana isn't authenticated!" How is your scripture authenticated? "Because we both accept it!" Then you didn't authenticate it from the start.

42. Give Mahayana that same faith and respect you're serving your texts. If something's true just because two parties accept it, we'd have to clock the Vedas as truth too.

43. If you're coming for Mahayana because it's controversial, throw out your own scripture - other groups are reading it for filth, and your own people are fighting about parts of it.

44. The teaching lives in the monkhood, but the monkhood isn't stable. For minds caught in grasping, even nirvana

---

[32] Four noble truths: Buddha's foundational teaching on: 1) the existence of suffering, 2) its causes, 3) the possibility of its cessation, and 4) the path leading to that cessation.

isn't giving stable energy.

45. If you think liberation comes right after eliminating mental afflictions, it should happen immediately. But we see karma still working those people who dropped their afflictions.

46. You think no craving means no grasping at rebirth? Why couldn't their craving exist as delusion, even without mental afflictions?

47. Craving comes from feeling, and they've got feeling. A mind with objects has to dwell on something.

48. Without emptiness, mind stays constrained and keeps coming back, like in non-cognitive meditation[33]. That's why you need to meditate on emptiness, darling.

49. If you're living for utterances that match the sutras as Buddha's words, why aren't you feeling the Mahayana that's mostly serving the same energy as your sutras?

50. If one bad part makes the whole thing wrong, why not consider it all Buddha's teaching when part of it matches the sutras?

51. If spiritual heavyweights like Maha-Kassapa[34] couldn't fully grasp these teachings, who are you to reject them just because your mind can't handle it?

52. Staying in this messy existence to help those confused and suffering? That happens through dropping attachment and fear - and that's what emptiness gives you, darling.

53. So there's no way to come for emptiness. Meditate on

---

[33] Non-cognitive meditation: Meditative states that lack discriminating wisdom, sometimes achieving calm but not insight into reality.

[34] Maha-Kassapa was one of the Buddha's foremost disciples, renowned for his austere practices and chosen to convene and lead the First Buddhist Council after the Buddha's death.

it without hesitation like it's your last chance at designer vintage.

54. Since emptiness is the ultimate read for the darkness of afflictions and obstacles to knowledge, why isn't everyone who wants omniscience meditating on it right this second?

55. Let fear come for things that actually cause suffering. Emptiness snatches suffering away - so why are you scared of it?

56. If there was actually something called "I," fear could come from anywhere. But if there's no "I," whose fear is it anyway?

57. Teeth, hair, nails? Not "I." Bone, blood, mucus, phlegm, pus, lymph? Still not "I," honey.

58. Body oil isn't "I," neither is sweat, fat, or entrails. The cavity where they sit isn't "I," and waste products definitely aren't "I."

59. Flesh isn't "I," neither are sinews, heat, or wind. Body openings aren't "I," and those six types of consciousness? Not "I" in any way, shape, or form.

60. If sound awareness was "I," you'd always be clocking sound. But without something to be aware of, what's it knowing that makes it awareness?

61. If something unconscious could be awareness, then this piece of wood I'm sitting on would be conscious. So clearly, there's no awareness without something to be aware of.

62. Why doesn't whatever knows form hear it too? "Because there's no sound to hear!" Please...

63. How can something that's essentially sound-awareness also be form-awareness? Someone can be both father and son, but not ultimately.

64. Since Sattva, Rajas, and Tamas aren't father or son material. Plus its nature has nothing to do with hearing sound.

65. If it's the same thing serving different looks like an actor, that's not permanent either. If it's got different natures, then this unity you're claiming is giving unprecedented delusion.

66. If another look isn't the real one, then spill the tea about its natural appearance. If awareness was its nature, then everyone would be identical.

67. Things with and without volition would be the same because their existence would be identical. If difference is false, what makes them similar?

68. What's not conscious isn't "I" because it's not conscious - like fabric and such. If it was consciousness because it has consciousness, then it would disappear when it stops being conscious.

69. If the self doesn't change, what's the point of its consciousness? That would mean space, with no consciousness or activity, has a self.

70. "Without a self, how can actions connect to results? If the action's doer is gone, who gets the result?"

71. When we both agree that actions and results have different bases and the self isn't involved, why are we still arguing about this?

72. Someone with the cause can't possibly have the result. The existence of the doer and experiencer depends on their consciousness stream being unified.

73. Past or future mind isn't "I" because it doesn't exist. If mind was "I," then when it vanishes, "I" would vanish too.

74. Like a banana tree trunk is nothing when cut up, the "I" doesn't exist when you analyze it.

75. "If no beings exist, who are you having compassion for?" For the ones imagined through delusion, which we accept to get things done.

76. "If there's no being, whose task is it?" True - the effort comes from delusion too. But to snatch away suffering, we don't block delusion about our task.

77. But grasping at "I" - which causes suffering - increases because of self-delusion. If that's unavoidable, then meditating on selflessness is the fiercest option.

78. The body isn't feet, calves, or thighs. It's not hips, abdomen, back, chest, or arms.

79. It's not hands, sides, armpits, or shoulders. It's not neck or head. So what here is actually body?

80. If this body exists partly in all these places, and its parts exist in their parts, where does it exist by itself?

81. If the whole body was in hands and other parts, we'd have as many bodies as we have hands and such.

82. Body isn't inside or outside. How can it be in hands and limbs? It's not separate from hands and such, so how can you find it at all?

83. So the body doesn't exist. But delusion makes us think we see a body in hands and such because of how they're arranged - like seeing a person in a pillar.

84. As long as conditions stay together, body appears like a person. Same way, as long as hands and such stay together, we keep seeing body there.

85. Same with foot - it's just toes assembled. Same with toes - they're just joints assembled. Same with joints - they're just their parts assembled.

86. Even parts break down into atoms, and atoms break down by directions. A direction section is just space because it

has no parts. So atoms don't exist either.

87. What queen with any sense would be attached to form that's just like a dream? If body doesn't exist, who's a woman and who's a man?

88. If suffering truly exists, why doesn't it come for happy people? If fancy food is pleasure, why doesn't it please someone serving grief realness?

89. If it's not experienced because something fiercer overshadows it, how can something that's not essentially experience be a feeling?

90. "But suffering exists in subtle form when the obvious form is gone." If it's just another pleasure, then that subtle state is subtle pleasure.

91. If suffering doesn't show up when its opposite's conditions arise, isn't "feeling" just a false concept we made up?

92. So this analysis is here to read that false notion for filth. The meditative states that come from investigation are what feed the contemplatives.

93. If there's space between sense faculty and object, where's the contact? If there's no space, they're identical - so what's contacting what?

94. One atom can't penetrate another because it has no empty space and they're the same size. No penetration means no mixing means no contact.

95. How can something without parts have contact? If you think part-less things can make contact, prove it.

96. Consciousness without form can't have contact, and neither can something composite because it doesn't truly exist, as we already read.

97. So if there's no contact, how can feeling arise? Why are we working so hard? What can harm what?

109

98. If there's no one experiencing feeling and feeling doesn't exist, then once you get this, why aren't you shattering, oh craving?

99. The dream-like, illusion-like mind sees and touches. Since feeling arises with mind, mind can't perceive it.

100. What happens earlier gets remembered but not experienced by what comes later. It doesn't experience itself, and nothing else experiences it either.

101. Nobody's experiencing feeling, darling. So really, there is no feeling. In this identity-less collection of parts, who's getting hurt by what?

102. Mind isn't in the sense organs, not in forms or other objects, not between them. It's not inside, outside, or anywhere else you look.

103. What's not in the body or anywhere else, not mixed in or separate - that's nothing. So beings are naturally liberated, honey.

104. If awareness comes before what it's aware of, what's it depending on to arise? If they show up together, what's it depending on then?

105. If it comes after what it's aware of, what's making awareness happen? This is how we know nothing truly comes into existence.

106. "If conventional truth isn't real, how can there be two truths? And if it exists because of another conventional truth, how can beings ever get liberated?"

107. One is someone else's mind making things up, and one doesn't exist by its own conventional truth. After something's verified, it exists; if not, it's not even conventionally real.

108. The concept and what's being conceived depend on each

other - just like every analysis uses what everyone already knows.

109. "But if you analyze using analysis that's been analyzed, it never ends because that analysis needs analyzing too."

110. When you analyze what's being analyzed, there's nothing left to analyze. No basis means nothing arises - and that's what we call nirvana, sweetie.

111. Someone who thinks these two truly exist is on shakier ground than a baby on stilts. If objects exist because cognition is serving power, how do you prove cognition truly exists?

112. If cognition exists from the object's power, how do you prove that? If they exist from each other's power, neither one can exist.

113. "If there's no father without a son, how can there be a son?" Just like no son means no father, neither of these exist.

114. "A sprout comes from a seed, and that seed is shown by the sprout. So why doesn't awareness arising from an object prove that object truly exists?"

115. We know a seed exists because of awareness that isn't the sprout. But how do you know awareness exists when the object is known by that same awareness?

116. People see every cause directly, like how lotus stalks and such come from various causes.

117. "What makes the causes various?" Previous various causes. "How does a cause give an effect?" Because of previous causes' power.

118. "God is the world's cause." Then spill the tea about who God is. If you mean the elements, fine - but why fight about a name?

119. Earth and other elements aren't one thing; they're imper-

QUEERING SHANTIDEVA'S THE WAY OF THE BODHISATTVA

manent, inactive, not divine. You can step on them and they're messy - that's not God.

120. Space isn't the Lord because it doesn't do anything. It's not the Self either, because we already read that for filth. How can you describe the inconceivable creating power of something inconceivable?

121. What's he trying to create? If he wants to create a self, aren't that self, the elements' nature, and God eternal? Awareness comes from objects and has no beginning.

122. Happiness and suffering come from actions. So what did he create? If the cause has no beginning, how can its effect have one?

123. If he doesn't depend on anything else, why isn't he always creating? If everything's created by him, what's he depending on?

124. If God depends on conditions coming together, then he's not the cause. He can't not create when conditions are there, and can't create when they're not.

125. If God creates without wanting to, he depends on something else. If he wants to create, he depends on that desire. Where's the creator's supremacy now?

126. We already read those "permanent atoms" for filth. The Samkhyas think there's some permanent primal substance causing the world.

127. The universal qualities - sattva, rajas, and tamas - in balance are called primal substance. They say the universe comes from them getting unbalanced.

128. One thing can't have three natures, so it doesn't exist. Same with these universal qualities - they'd each need three qualities themselves.

129. Without these three universal qualities, how can sound

and other sense objects exist? And unconscious things like fabric can't have pleasure and such.

130. If you're saying things have the nature of causes, haven't we already analyzed that away? For you, pleasure and such are the cause, but fabric and such aren't their result.

131. Happiness and other feelings might come from things like fabric, but without them, there'd be no happiness. The permanence of happiness and feelings is never proven.

132. If happiness manifesting truly exists, why can't you perceive the feeling? If you say it becomes subtle, how can it be both obvious and subtle?

133. "It gets subtle when it leaves its obvious state. Its obvious and subtle states aren't permanent." Why not see everything as impermanent that way?

134. If its obvious state isn't different from happiness, then happiness is clearly impermanent. If you think something non-existent doesn't arise because it doesn't exist at all, then you've accidentally accepted that something manifest can come from nothing.

135. If you think the effect is already in the cause, then eating food would be eating waste, and you'd buy cotton seeds at cloth prices and wear them.

136. If you say regular folks don't see this because they're confused, that applies to those who know reality too.

137. Even regular folks know that. Why don't they see it? If you say regular folks have no verifying awareness, then even their perception of obvious things is false.

138. "If verifying awareness isn't verifying awareness, is what's not verified false? Actually, emptiness of phenomena isn't verified through that awareness."

139. You can't understand that something doesn't exist without

113

first imagining that thing. So if something is false/illusory, saying "it doesn't exist" is also false.

140. Here's an example. Let's say you have no children. If, then, you dream that your son has died, thinking "he doesn't exist" actually requires first thinking about his existence. And that thought of non-existence is also false. Both the existence and non-existence are mental constructs.

141. This leads to: nothing exists independently. Everything depends on causes and conditions - either individually or in combination with other things.

142. Nothing truly comes from somewhere else, nothing truly stays around forever, and nothing truly disappears. What's the difference between an illusion and what confused people think is real?

143. Look at this: What's created by illusion and what's created by causes - where do they come from and where do they go?

144. How can something artificial like a reflection be truly real when you only see it with something else, never by itself? Make it make sense!

145. If something already exists, why does it need a cause? If it doesn't exist, what's a cause going to do for it?

146. Something non-existent won't change even with millions of causes throwing shade. How can that be called existence? What else could possibly come into being?

147. If nothing exists when something doesn't exist, when will existence show up? That non-existence isn't going anywhere until existence gets produced.

148. When non-existence is still serving, there's no room for existence to werk. And something existing can't become non-existent - that would mean it's serving two natures

at once.

149. So nothing ever stops or starts existing. Which means this whole world neither arises nor ceases - and that's the tea.

150. States of existence are giving dream realness. Analyze them and they're like banana trees - all show, no substance. Really, there's no difference between those who've reached nirvana and those who haven't.

151. When everything's empty like this, what's there to gain or lose? Who's getting praised or dragged, and by whom?

152. Where's happiness or suffering coming from? What's good and what's bad? When you investigate its true nature, what is craving and what's it craving?

153. Look deeper - what is this world of living beings? Who's really dying here? Who's coming into existence, who's already here, who's related to whom, and who's really friends with anyone?

154. May everyone like me see everything as empty as space. They're raging and rejoicing over arguments and celebrations.

155. Chasing their own happiness through messy deeds, they're living that miserable life with grief, problems, despair, and hurting each other.

156. They keep getting reborn in fortunate realms, getting used to pleasure again and again, then dying and falling into miserable states with long, intense suffering.

157. There are so many traps in worldly existence, but this truth isn't one of them. Things contradict each other - reality can't be like this.

158. There are incomparable, fierce, endless oceans of suffering. Strength is scarce and life is short.

159. Even there, in practices for long life and health, in hunger,

exhaustion and tiredness, in sleep and disasters, and in worthless connections with fools...

160. Life passes faster than last season's trends, and for nothing. It's hard to get wisdom - how can you stop those habitual distractions?

161. There too, Mara's[35] trying to throw them into the messiest states. With so many wrong paths, doubt is harder to overcome than a bad hair day.

162. And this precious human life is hard to get. A Buddha showing up is rarer than a perfect thrift store find. The flood of mental afflictions is harder to stop than gossip. Girl, what a mess of suffering!

163. Oh, we should feel such compassion for those drowning in suffering's flood, who are so messy but don't even know how messy their situation is.

164. Like someone who keeps dunking themselves in water but has to jump in fire again and again - they think they're fortunate when they're actually serving pure suffering.

165. Living like aging and death won't come for them, terrible disasters show up with death leading the parade.

166. So when can I bring relief to those tormented by suffering's fire, with happiness springing from my merit clouds like a surprise production number?

167. When can I teach emptiness and merit-gathering with respect (in conventional terms, without making it too real) to those whose views are too solid?

---

[35] Mara: The personification of destructive forces in Buddhism, often depicted as a demonic figure who tried to prevent the Buddha from achieving enlightenment. Represents obstacles to spiritual practice.

10. Dedication

1. May every single being get find their way to strut down this same spiritual runway, through all this inner work I've done composing this guide to living that fierce bodhisattva life,

2. By all this goodness I've created, may everyone who's suffering - body, mind, or spirit - find themselves swimming in oceans of pure joy, living their best authentic lives.

3. For as long as this cosmic ball keeps spinning, honey, may their happiness never fade like last season's trends. May the whole world get a taste of that eternal bodhisattva bliss.

4. For all those trapped in personal hells - and baby, we've all been there - may they suddenly find themselves transported to pure pleasure paradise, where every day is like Pride with zero drama.

5. For anyone feeling that cold shoulder from life, may they find warmth. And for those burning up with life's heat, may the blessed bodhisattvas rain down cooling relief like the world's fiercest sprinkler system.

6. Where there's nothing but thorns and sharp edges cutting deep, may pleasure gardens bloom. Where life's been

harsh and unforgiving, may wish-fulfilling trees spring up serving pure abundance.

7. May every hellish situation transform into a fabulous oasis, complete with lotus-filled pools and the sweet songs of gorgeous birds living their best lives.

8. Where there's nothing but burning wreckage, let crystal palaces rise. Where mountains of suffering crush spirits, let temples of pure light emerge, filled with enlightened beings serving face and wisdom.

9. Where it's raining pain and daggers, let it rain flower petals instead. And where there's nothing but fights and drama, let there be playful competitions where everybody wins.

10. For all those stripped down to bare bones, swimming in rivers of fire - honey, we see you - may they work that glow-up into celestial bodies and find themselves lounging by heavenly streams with divine companions.

11. Let all those scary forces of death and decay suddenly get shook when they see that fierce protector Vajrapani serving electric realness in the sky. When they see that light that snatches all shadows, may they wonder "Who is she?" and follow that queen right into liberation.

12. As lotus petals rain down with sacred waters, putting out the flames of suffering, may all those trapped in personal hells feel that sudden rush of joy and catch sight of Avalokiteshvara, the original queen of compassion.

13. Come through, family! Don't be scared - we're living! That radiant prince in monk's robes just showed up to snatch us all into liberation. Watch how he removes every obstacle, gets those joy juices flowing, and births both enlightenment and fierce compassion in our hearts.

14. Look at this divine queen Manjushri, with gods laid

118

prostrate at his lotus feet, tears of compassion giving him that eternal glow, flower petals raining on that crown, surrounded by thousands of divine beings singing his praises. The moment those in hell catch this lewk, may they feel nothing but pure joy.

15. Through all this good jush I've built up, may everyone stuck in their personal hells look up and see nothing but clouds of bodhisattvas, led by that legendary child Samantabhadra, bringing sweet cooling rain and gentle breezes.

16. May all the intense suffering and paralyzing fears of those in hell just evaporate. May everyone stuck in miserable situations find their way to freedom faster than you can say "sashay away."

17. May we end this cycle of beings eating each other - it's giving very that. And may the hungry ghosts find themselves living as lavishly as the most fortunate beings in existence.

18. May those hungry ghosts always be fed and refreshed by streams of milk flowing from Avalokiteshvara's hands - serving sustenance and liberation, honey!

19. May the blind see all this beauty, may the deaf hear all this truth, and may pregnant women give birth as easily as Maya did[36] - no muss, no fuss, just pure miracle.

20. May everyone get exactly what their heart desires and what their spirit needs - fierce outfits, nourishing food, refreshing drinks, flower crowns, that good sandalwood

---

[36] Maya: OG Buddha's birth mother, referenced here regarding her legendary painless delivery of the Buddha. According to tradition, she gave birth standing up, holding onto a sal tree branch.

perfume, and all the accessories that make life divine.

21. Let the scared find their courage, let the grieving find their joy. May the depressed find their fire and those shaking in their boots find their strength.

22. May sick bodies find healing, may chains of all kinds break and fall away. May the weak discover their power, and may everyone's hearts open to each other with pure love.

23. May every journey be smooth for all the travelers out there. May everyone reach their destination and accomplish exactly what they set out to do.

24. For all those sailing life's waters, may they reach their shores safely and celebrate with their loved ones - chosen family included, darling.

25. For anyone lost in dark places, may they find their tribe of fellow travelers. May their journey be free from danger - no shady characters, no fierce beasts, nothing but safe passage.

26. May divine protection wrap around the confused, the mentally ill, the overwhelmed, the helpless, the young and old, the sick, and anyone lost in life's wilderness.

27. May everyone find time and space to practice, filled with faith, wisdom, and compassion. May they serve elegance and good behavior, and may they remember all their past lives like they're binge-watching their own reality show.

28. May they become endless sources of abundance, like treasures falling from the sky. Free from drama and irritation, may they live independently and authentically.

29. May those serving basic realness be blessed with magnificent sparkle. May those feeling ugly and rejected discover their inner and outer beauty.

30. May everyone express their true gender freely. May those

feeling low rise up high, but keep their egos in check - nobody likes a diva with a bad attitude.

31. Through all this spiritual werk I've done, may every single being drop their messy habits and start serving pure virtue instead.

32. Never losing that awakened spirit, devoted to the bodhisattva path, held in the Buddhas' embrace, and free from all that demon drama.

33. May everyone live forever and ever. May they stay happy as can be, and may we forget that death is even a thing.

34. May the whole world transform into a pleasure garden with wish-fulfilling trees everywhere, filled with Buddhas and their fierce children, everything elegant with the sound of sacred teachings.

35. May the ground everywhere be smooth as a baby's bottom, soft and lovely, made of pure lapis lazuli - we're talking luxury, darling.

36. May crowds of bodhisattvas work it on all sides, making this earth even more gorgeous with their radiant realness.

37. May everyone hear the Dharma being spilled constantly - from the birds, from the trees, from rays of light, from the sky itself - the ultimate surround sound system.

38. May everyone constantly run into Buddhas and their children out there living their best lives. May they shower their spiritual mentors with endless offerings - make it rain, honey!

39. May the rains come right on schedule, may the crops be abundant, may everyone prosper, and may the rulers actually serve justice - imagine that!

40. May all medicines do their job, may all mantras come through with power, and may all those scary spirits and

ghouls get touched by compassion and switch teams.

41. May nobody have to deal with unhappiness, mess, illness, neglect, or shade. May nobody ever feel hopeless about their situation. May all spiritual centers be thriving, full of study and sacred sounds.

42. May all spiritual communities live in harmony, and may they accomplish everything they're meant to do. May all monks seeking to practice find their quiet spots.

43. May they meditate with sharp minds, unbothered by any distractions - pure focus, honey. May all nuns get their needs met and stay free from drama and trouble.

44. May everyone who renounces worldly life keep their ethics clean and pristine.

45. For those struggling with their ethical commitments, may they get fed up with their own mess and focus on cleaning up their act. May they level up to better circumstances and keep their vows unbroken.

46. May they become educated and cultured, receive what they need, and stay provided for. May their minds flow pure and clean, and may their good reputation spread in all directions like a viral moment.

47. Without having to experience the rough stuff or practice till they drop, may everyone wake up to their Buddha nature in this divine body they're wearing right now.

48. May all beings worship all the Buddhas in countless fierce ways. May they experience joy beyond imagination, tasting that inconceivable Buddha bliss.

49. May all the bodhisattvas' wishes to help the world come true. Whatever these protectors intend for beings, may it all manifest exactly as planned.

50. May the solo practitioners and disciples stay happy, always

getting their life from gods, antigods[37], and humans who know how to show proper respect.

51. Through Manjushri's blessing, may I always get to be a monastic and remember all my past lives until I reach that Joyous Ground[38] - level up!

52. May I stay fierce and fabulous no matter what kind of situation life throws my way. In all my lifetimes, may I find those perfect peaceful spots to get my meditation on without the drama.

53. Whenever I need guidance or have questions, may I see my spiritual guides with no barriers, no waiting list.

54. May I serve it like Manjushri does, living that life dedicated to helping every single being get their glow-up across all directions.

55. As long as there's space to exist in and worlds to work with, may I stay clearing away all the world's suffering.

56. Whatever mess the world is going through, may it all come to me instead - I'll take those hits. May the whole world find its joy through the fierce energy of all the bodhisattvas.

57. May the dharma - that one perfect prescription for all the world's suffering and the source of all its sickening success - stay around for ages, getting all the coin and recognition

---

[37] Antigods (asuras) are powerful, jealous deities who are constantly fighting with the gods due to their competitiveness and pride - think of them as the drama queens of the higher realms. This keeps the hierarchy clear: gods, antigods, and humans are all potential supporters of dharma practitioners, each bringing their own fierce energy to the spiritual scene.

[38] The Joyous Ground (Pramudita) is the first of the ten bodhisattva levels, marked by overwhelming joy at beginning to realize emptiness while perfecting generosity.

it deserves.

58. I'm bowing down to Manjushri, whose blessing makes my mind turn to virtue like a sunflower to the light. And I'm giving props to my spiritual bestie, whose kindness makes me strong.

III

The Aftermath

In Conclusion

Picture it: The sun was high over Nalanda, the crowd was gagged, and Shantideva was just flowing through chapter after chapter of pure spiritual wisdom, serving looks that could kill delusion and dropping truth bombs that would make even the shadiest monks stop and think.

According to Tibetan legend, when he reached Chapter 9 - the one about wisdom and emptiness - that things got really fierce. As he began to explain the deepest nature of reality, our boy started to rise from his throne. And not in a "let me stand up for emphasis" way. I'm talking full-on levitation, floating higher and higher until he straight-up disappears into the sky. But they could still hear his voice coming down from above. As he concluded his performance, he gently floated back down to the crowd and had everyone speechless.

Now that's what I call a mic drop.

What makes this story so important isn't just the magical elements (though honey, those are fierce). It's that Shantideva was teaching us something profound about authenticity and appearances. Here was someone who looked like a mess on the outside but was cultivating incredible wisdom on the inside. Sound familiar? It's like every queer person who ever had to hide their true self while developing their inner strength. His masterpiece isn't just some dusty old text - it's a revolutionary manifesto about transforming yourself through compassion and wisdom. It's about seeing through the drama of everyday life to find something deeper and more meaningful. It's about being fierce in your dedication to helping others, even when nobody understands what you're doing.

Shantideva's work has been spilling the tea on spiritual transformation for over 1,200 years now. The Dalai Lama teaches from it regularly. It's been translated into more languages than Madonna has reinvented herself. And its message about combining wisdom with compassion is more relevant than ever.

Think about it: Here was someone who gave up every privilege, faced ridicule and shade, and still came through with more grace than a ballroom legend. Why? Because he understood that true happiness isn't about external validation - it's about transforming your mind and helping others.

So why should we care about this ancient Indian prince-turned-monk in our modern queer lives? Because honey, Shantideva's story and teachings speak to us on levels deeper than your most introspective 3 AM social media posts.

First off, let's talk about authenticity. Shantideva chose to live his truth even when it meant disappointing every single expectation his family and society had for him. Sound familiar? It's like coming out times ten - not just about your identity, but about your whole way of being in the world. He showed us that sometimes you have to let people think you're a mess while you're doing your inner work. (And isn't that just the perfect metaphor for those awkward years of questioning your gender or sexuality?)

Then there's his teachings about compassion. In "Guide to

128

the Bodhisattva's Way of Life," he spills the tea about how to genuinely care for others without burning yourself out - something every queer activist needs to hear. He taught that real compassion comes from wisdom, not just emotional reaction. It's like understanding the difference between posting a rainbow flag during Pride month and actually showing up for trans youth all year round.

But perhaps his most radical teaching was about emptiness: the ultimate nature of reality. Now, before you roll your eyes thinking this is some abstract philosophical nonsense, listen up! Shantideva was basically teaching that nothing exists in the solid, fixed way we think it does. Including gender. Including sexuality. Including all the boxes society tries to put us in. When he talks about seeing through appearances to the deeper nature of reality, he's giving us tools to dismantle not just heteronormativity, but all the ways we get stuck in limiting beliefs about ourselves and others. It's like gender theory meets Buddhist philosophy, but make it practical.

So how do we work with Shantideva's teachings today? Start by approaching your own path with the same authenticity he showed. Maybe you're not ready to float away during a teaching, but you can be real about where you're at and what you're working on. Take his teachings on patience when dealing with haters (and honey, he had some things to say about that). He taught that those who oppose us are actually helping us develop strength - like emotional resistance training. Next time someone's serving ignorance, remember you're getting a free workout for your compassion muscles. And most importantly, remember his message about combining wisdom with compassion.

In our community, we need both - the wisdom to see through

societal conditioning and the compassion to help others who are still struggling with it. Shantideva's story reminds us that sometimes the most revolutionary act is simply being true to your path, even when others don't understand it. He showed us that real transformation doesn't always look Instagram-worthy from the outside, and that's okay.

So the next time you're feeling misunderstood, or like your spiritual path is taking you in directions your friends don't get, remember our boy Shantideva. Remember that sometimes the ones they call lazy or weird or too much are the ones who end up changing the world. After all, as Shantideva might say if he were here today: "Let them think what they want - you focus on developing that bodhisattva mind, queen."

* * *

Let's dive deeper into how Shantideva's teachings can apply to our fabulous queer lives:

Compassion for Ourselves: Shantideva teaches us to cultivate compassion for all beings, and honey, that includes ourselves. In a world that often tells us we're wrong or broken, practicing self-compassion is a radical act. It's like being your own fairy godmother, waving that wand of kindness over your own heart.

Patience with Our Journey: Coming out, transitioning, finding our place in the community - these processes take time. Shantideva's teachings on patience remind us that it's okay to take things one fabulous step at a time. Your journey is your own, and it's not a race.

130

Enthusiasm for Activism: Shantideva's chapter on enthusiasm can fuel our fight for equality. It's a reminder that every small action counts, whether it's attending a Pride parade or having a heartfelt conversation with a family member who doesn't understand.

Wisdom in Identity: The teachings on emptiness can help us navigate the complex world of gender and sexuality. Labels can be useful tools, but they're not the totality of who we are. We're as fluid and boundless as the cosmos itself, darling.

Generosity in Community: Shantideva emphasizes the importance of giving. In our community, this can manifest as mentoring younger LGBTQ+ folks, volunteering at queer organizations, or simply being there for a friend in need.

Ethical Living in a Complex World: The bodhisattva vows give us a framework for ethical living that goes beyond societal norms. It's about doing what's truly kind and beneficial, not just what's expected. Meditation for Mental Health: In a community that faces higher rates of anxiety and depression, Shantideva's teachings on meditation offer valuable tools for mental wellbeing. It's like a spa day for your mind, honey.

Transforming Discrimination: Shantideva teaches us to transform adverse circumstances into the path. This means we can use experiences of discrimination as opportunities to cultivate compassion and work towards change.

Interconnectedness in Diversity: The concept of emptiness teaches us that we're all interconnected. In the diverse spectrum

131

of our community, this reminds us that our liberation is bound up with everyone else's.

Dedication of Merit: By dedicating the merit of our actions to all beings, we expand our impact beyond ourselves. Every time we stand up for our rights, we're standing up for everyone's rights.

Now, let's talk about how Shantideva's teachings can help us navigate some of the unique challenges our queer community faces: D

Dealing with Homophobia and Transphobia: Shantideva's teachings on patience and compassion give us tools to deal with discrimination without losing our fabulous selves in the process. It's like having an emotional shield that deflects hate while radiating fabulousness.

Coming Out: The bodhisattva path is all about authenticity and courage. Sound familiar? Coming out is a bodhisattva move, honey. You're not just being true to yourself, you're helping create a more accepting world for others.

Body Image Issues: In a community that often places a high value on physical appearance, Shantideva's teachings on the nature of reality can be liberating. Your body is just your current outfit, darling. Your true self is so much more fabulous and expansive.

Chosen Family Dynamics: Shantideva's emphasis on compassion and patience can help us navigate the complex relationships in our chosen families. It's like having a guidebook for building and maintaining your queer support network.

Activism Burnout: The bodhisattva path is a marathon, not a sprint. Shantideva's teachings can help us stay committed to the fight for equality while also taking care of ourselves. It's like learning how to be a diva on stage and a zen master backstage.

Dating and Relationships: Emptiness teachings can liberate us from unrealistic expectations in relationships. Plus, Shantideva's advice on patience and compassion? Relationship gold, honey.

Intersectionality: Shantideva's vision of universal compassion aligns beautifully with intersectional approaches to LGBTQ+ activism. It's about lifting everyone up, not just those who look or love like us.

HIV/AIDS and Health: For a community that's been deeply impacted by the HIV/AIDS crisis, Shantideva's teachings on impermanence and the preciousness of human life can be particularly poignant. It's a reminder to live fully and love fiercely, no matter what.

Queer Joy: Sometimes, in the face of challenges, we forget to celebrate our fabulousness. Shantideva's teachings on rejoicing remind us to revel in the beauty of our community and our individual journeys.

Spiritual Reconciliation: For those of us who've felt rejected by traditional religions, Shantideva offers a spiritual path that celebrates compassion and authenticity. It's like finding a spiritual home that loves you exactly as you are.

As we wrap up this deep dive into Shantideva's world, let's take a moment to appreciate the fabulousness of this spiritual journey we're on. Shantideva shows us that being spiritual doesn't mean being somber or boring. It's about living life fully, loving fiercely, and serving compassion realness every day.

Remember, darlings, in the words of Shantideva himself: "For as long as space endures and for as long as living beings remain, until then may I too abide to dispel the misery of the world." It's like he's encouraging us to be the glitter in the darkness, the rainbow after the storm.

So, my beautiful queer family, are you ready to walk the bodhisattva path? Are you prepared to turn your compassion up to eleven and your ego down to zero? Remember, in the immortal words of Shantideva (as interpreted by your truly): "If you can love yourself and everyone else, honey, you're already halfway to enlightenment."

In the grand show of life, we're all here to help each other shine. So spread that bodhichitta energy like it's glitter, and let's make this world a more fabulous place for everyone. Shantideva would be proud, darling.

Discover the
Queering the Path to Enlightenment
Series!

Living for this spiritual glow-up? Meet us on the path...
Books One and Two - AVAILABLE NOW!

Start your journey with an introduction to Buddhist basics that speaks your language. Learn how Buddha and Atisha were serving revolutionary realness centuries before Stonewall. Find out why this ancient wisdom hits different for queer folks today.

From DRAMA to Dharma

Compassion That Walk!

Compassion That Walk! takes you deeper into the Buddhist path through stories of legendary spiritual revolutionaries like Shantideva and Milarepa. Experience profound teachings about transformation, authenticity, and the power of compassion in action.

But Why Wait?!

Turn the page for an exclusive preview of Book Two, where you'll meet Shantideva - the originl spiritual underdog who went from serving lazy realness to floating through the ceiling while spitting pure wisdom. (hey, you just read that!)

Join our chosen sangha as we make Buddhist wisdom accessible, authentic, and fiercely relevant.

Because this path is for everyone, darling - especially those of us who had to find our own way home.

About David Franklin Sparks

Let me spill some tea about our fierce author, David Franklin Sparks! This multifaceted queen isn't just serving one type of realness - he's a Buddhist practitioner, writer, musician, and drag performer who knows how to werk it in multiple venues, honey. As the musical artist dFRAE and the drag persona Fancy Sparkles, David brings creativity and authenticity to everything he touches. But his true passion? Making Buddhist teachings accessible and relevant to the LGBTQ+ community. After years of studying and practicing Buddhism while navigating queer life, David saw the need for a spiritual guide that spoke our language. That's what led him to write "Queering the Path to Enlightenment," bringing together his love for Buddhism and his commitment to the LGBTQ+ community. When he's not busy making the Dharma fabulous or producing indie pop bops, David's probably somewhere being his full grown self.